THE CHURCH'S HISTORY OF INJUSTICE AND WHY THIS PRIEST LEFT

John F. Sheehy

University Press of America,® Inc.
Lanham • New York • Oxford

Copyright © 1999
University Press of America,® Inc.
4720 Boston Way
Lanham, Maryland 20706

12 Hid's Copse Rd.
Cumnor Hill, Oxford OX2 9JJ

All rights reserved
Printed in the United States of America
British Library Cataloging in Publication Information Available

Library of Congress Cataloging-in-Publication Data

Sheehy, John F.
The Church's history of injustice and why this priest left / John F. Sheehy.
p. cm.
1. Catholic Church—Controversial literature. 2. Christianity and justice—Catholic Church. 3. Church and social problems—Catholic Church—History. 4. Catholic Church—Clergy. 5. Celibacy—Catholic Church. 6. Civil rights—Religious aspects—Catholic Church. 7. Sheehy, John F. I. Title.
BX1765.2.S44   1998   261.7'088'22—dc21   98-48435 CIP

ISBN 0-7618-1310-1 (pbk: alk. ppr.)

∞™ The paper used in this publication meets the minimum requirements of American National Standard for Information Sciences—Permanence of Paper for Printed Library Materials, ANSI Z39.48—1984

ACKNOWLEDGMENTS

I never would have gotten a clear understand of the patriarchy or the subjection of women without the constant prodding of my wife, Sonja Rae. It was her interest in the Church that brought us together and our continual discussion of the Church, politics, the subjection of women that led to my critical examination of the Church. Without her I never would have made the journey.

Besides, I am indebted to the Civil Rights Movement of the sixties, which helped lead me to freedom. My mentor, Dr. James Jackson shared a great part in this milestone. My son, Scott Randall Sheehy, was my first typist and I probably would not have begun this project unless he offered to begin the typing, so I thank him and my middle and ending typists, Lee Ann Wall, who typed the whole manuscript and Donna Smith-Hunsley, who added the final touches.

I bounced many of my ideas off two clergymen friends, Larry Dannemiller and Bob Cunningham. The are friends over decades. I had two great editors and critics; Wanda Brandstetter and Valia Herschi, two wise women whose input I treasure.

Also I wish to thank Georgette Senter for getting the manuscript camera ready.

The author gratefully acknowledges permission to reprint portions of the following copyrighted material: From A Basic Call to Consciousness, The Hau De Nu Sauc Nee Address to the Western World, published by Akwesaue Notes initially delivered at the United Nations Conference on Indigenous Peoples.

Although I am highly critical of the Church, I would never have made this journey without the Church. The great ides of Jesus about love, poverty and social justice captivated me and without the Church I might not have been exposed to these ideas or seen the contradictions in the system. I never would have met my wife!

I believe with Dietrich Bonhoffer that the greatest obstacle to Christianity is Religion, but I want to thank all those persons of religion or of Christianity that engaged me in dialogue and taught me the elusiveness of truth, which is never attained but must be constantly pursued.

TABLE OF CONTENTS

Introduction		1
Chapter 1	The Early Practices of the Church	5
Chapter 2	How the Early Church Handled Heresy and Deviants	11
Chapter 3	Prejudice Toward Marriage (As Taught by Jerome, Augustine, Origen, Popes)	19
Chapter 4	The Imposition of Celibacy (An Infringement on Human Rights)	25
Chapter 5	The Church as a Civil Power	29
Chapter 6	The Crusades (An Abuse of Civil Rights)	33
Chapter 7	The Inquisition (A WORD THAT STILL STRIKES TERROR IN OUR HEARTS)	39
Chapter 8	The Reformation Reduction of Rights by Catholics and Protestants - The Huguenots	47
Chapter 9	Biblical Inquiry and Human Rights	53
Chapter 10	The Use of the "Natural Law" to Continue Bondage	59

Chapter 11	Slavery and the Church	65
Chapter 12	The American Indians and Christianity	71
Chapter 13	Present Attitude of the Church and Women's Rights	79
Chapter 14	Homosexuality and the Church Today	85
Chapter 15	The Civil Rights Movement of the Sixties (As Seen in Muskegon, MI)	91
Chapter 16	What is the Major Problem Caused by the Denial of Human Rights?	111
Chapter 17	What Can the Church do to Further Human Rights? Will They?	117
Chapter 18	Summary and Epilogue The Church-An Out Moded Paradigm	125

INTRODUCTION

THE CHURCH AND CIVIL RIGHTS

Recalling the attitude of the Catholic Church, specifically, during the sixties, prompted me to think and write about the general position of the Church on these and similar issues. For a long time I have been aware that the Church was (and is) hung up on sex. One would think an institution of this kind would be geared more toward human and civil rights than to sex. But the Church is not, has not, and maybe never will be Civil Rights oriented.

The United States is witnessing a renewal of hostility and bias toward blacks, Jews, women and homosexuals to name only a few of the many groups. Obviously this is not a rational problem that can be refuted by facts, data and/or argumentation. People who propose views that separate humans and teach them bias and hatred toward other human beings need to be isolated and named a threat to humanity.

The Church is not on the side of the oppressed, is not actively engaged in eliminating racism, sexism and homophobia. The Church is part of the problem. The Church has actively persecuted Jews, Heretics, Moslems, women through its whole existence and continues to do so.

It is time for the Church to be exposed for what it is, a purveyor of prejudice, hostility and hypocrisy. Of course the Church has done many good things in its history and has fostered holiness in many of its members. It has helped the orphan and sheltered the homeless. It has taught the teachings of Jesus, has preserved the Scriptures and has produced many models of the good life. Yet, along with these and other acts and institutions the Church has relegated women to second-class citizenship because they do not have penises. The church presently, and its antiquated notions on homosexuality, is ready to dig in again, as it did at the time of Galileo on the side of ignorance and to help foster prejudice against homosexuals and thus help make it possible for the United States officially to practice discrimination in the name of truth, God, and the Church.

United States Senators Sam Nunn and Daniel Coats come from a long line of officials, taught and led by the Church, who now try to control the progress of our nation by tethering its energies in a non-problem, sexual preference which is not preference but genetic. If the Church, Catholic and Protestant would speak out on these and similar issues we could concentrate on some real problems: poverty, homelessness, drugs, gangs, jobs, and health.

Perhaps many people reading what I write, will become hostile. I don't blame them, since I am questioning the innate goodness of an institution that many have been taught to love from birth. Many look to the Church for solace in times of trouble, for grace to combat the struggles of life, and for the promise of salvation.

Perhaps the Church has and will continue to perform these services, but the Church, like business, government, education, and the military, needs periodically to examine its own first principles, rewrite them and move on. It took the Church over three hundred years to face up to Galileo. How long will it take for it to face up to its attitude on women and homosexuals?

The Catholic Bishops of the United States have been trying to issue a pastoral letter on women for about eight years (1996). They can't bring themselves to say that women are basically inferior because they don't have penises. Isn't that the nub of the affair? For years women and men believed women were inferior. That's the way God intended it. Of course God never said any such thing, but if some of his regulations about uncleanness in the Old Testament are taken as direct quotes from God, we might wonder about him or her.

Jesus never said women were inferior. He spent plenty of time with women. The Samaritan woman was a missionary for Jesus. She wondered about him too, his carefree attitude toward women. Women stayed with Jesus until the end of his life and were the first witnesses of the Resurrection. He became flesh through a woman. Isn't this enough so called proof? But no, since the Pope says there were no women at the Last Supper. Someone pointed out in a letter to Time, "There were not Polish people there either.

Let's face it, there is no theological reason why women can't be ordained priests. When we say the Church is unchangeable what exactly do we mean? Some of the things Jerome, Augustine, Origen, and Aquinas said were appalling.[1]

---

[1] Since these names appear frequently in the text, I will briefly explain who they are here.

Jerome (340-420 CE) translated the Old and New Testament into Latin. This was referred to as The

Vulgate since it put the scriptures into common parlance. The Vulgar language. He appears to have

been terrified of women, though he lived off their beneficence.

Augustine (354-430) originally a free spirited liver who fathered an illegitimate child, then converted to

Christianity, advocated celibacy and spurning women. He had tremendous influence on the church

leaders and his teaching on sin still scares millions. His perverse attitude about women has lead the

Church in the wrong direction since he wrote his confessions and the City of God.

Origen: (185-230) early Christian biblical scholar and theologian, also obsessed with the dangers of sex and proved it by castrating himself.

Aquinas: (1225-1276) Author of the <u>Summa Theological</u>, A Summary of Christian teaching integrated with the Philosophy of Aristotle. St. Thomas's great and sweeping view of dogma and morality seems marred by his attitude toward women, based on errors by Aristotle, Augustine and his mentor St. Albert the Great. It is unfortunate that many Roman Catholic theologians and Popes cannot embrace Aquinas in many teachings and openly renounce his obvious errors.

CHAPTER 1

THE EARLY PRACTICES
OF THE CHURCH

The Church, also called the assembly, has always been exclusive, although its mission is to include everybody. The Church would certainly accept all that came, provided they follow the rules and procedures.

The trouble is not everyone is willing to come, and *if* they do come, will they listen to the proclamations, profess faith in Jesus, join with the faithful in the Eucharist and the fellowship of love? "By this shall all men know that you are my disciples, because you love one another."

The Christian Church was preceded by its historical and religious ancestor, Judaism. All the earliest Christians were Jews, and of course Jesus and the apostles were Jews. When the followers of Jesus began to preach salvation through Jesus they went first to the Jews. They preached in the synagogues of the Jews, as recorded in Acts.

They assumed that the Jews would be delighted to hear about the saving death and resurrection of Jesus and would profess faith. The transition from Judaism to Christianity could have been easy and almost unnoticeable. Many of them did accept Jesus, but many did not. This astounded the early preachers, particularly Paul, who had already become the apostle of the Gentiles. The apostles gradually gave up on preaching to the Jews and using their synagogues. Slowly they broke away from Jewish rites, like circumcision. They changed the day of official worship from Saturday to Sunday and even changed their diet.

The first day was the day of the resurrection and it seemed only natural to celebrate this day rather than Saturday. It was not such a big shift because the vigil of the return of Jesus began on Saturday. This too, distinguished the Christians from the Jews, especially in the eyes of the Romans who gradually became aware that the Christians were a different group from the Jews.

These early and naturally separations gradually led to some ill feeling between the Christians and the Jews. After all, if I came to you with a message of salvation, for your own good of course, and you rejected me, I would wonder about whether you were an open person, maybe not even worthy of salvation. The division begins.

These divisions have afflicted humanity from prehistoric times. People of different tribes, skin colors, languages, with different tools, skills, beliefs and gods have mystified others who came across them from the beginning. The Jews discovered that the Babylonians were astute builders, with a greatly advanced civilization. They built ziggurats. The Jews referred to one of those as the tower of Babel and even projected that their discovery of different languages was explainable by God, deliberately confusing the builders who apparently were trying to reach the heavens.

The Jews also discovered there were some people larger than themselves. They were giants and they explained this by saying these could have come only from a bad source, the cohabitation of evil spirits with the daughters of men. They didn't know about dietary influence and genes in those days.

Also, the Jews did not think much of their neighbors in Canaan especially the Moabites and the Ammorites. They then explained their origins as coming from the incestuous relationship from Lot's daughters with Lot. Where else would such people come from? And this reinforced the Jewish aversion for intermarriage with these peoples. They thought this also brought contamination, alien practices, strange beliefs, and strange gods. Even Solomon, the wise man, was lead astray by his many wives from alien groups.

The Christians inherited much of this spirit of being wary of outsiders, non-believers, and alien groups. Even the Jews became an alien group and soon it appeared they were unworthy even in the scriptures.

The New Testament was composed between twenty and eighty years after Christ. The gospels were not all written at the same time and many followed later after the writings of Paul. By this time the apostles had given up on trying to convert Jews to Christianity. They didn't reject the Jews but they found that proselytizing them only upset and turned them away.

Mohammed[2] would discover this five hundred years later. The great Arab reformer thought that if he indicated to the Jews and Christians that his monotheism was the essence of religion, that the world center of religion was Mecca, not Rome or Jerusalem, other groups would welcome the news and regroup with Islam. Some did, but most did not. Mohammed then gradually became hostile to Jews and Christians and although he did not preach bigotry and hate, he frequently did point out that the future of Jews and Christians was dim.

The animosities of religious groups toward one another afflicts us today in Northern Ireland, India, Pakistan, Bosnia, everywhere. Deliberately or not, religion has divided us, one from the other. And as we see others as different, unworthy, less chosen in the eyes of God, we easily turn to avoiding these people, not communicating with them, finally frequently depriving them of their rights and persecuting them. May be in the name of god and religion.

To return to the New Testament, we can see, that as the apostles and their followers began to tell the story of Jesus and his message many years after it happened, they put in items to clarify the message and to update the happenings. After all, they were writing out of several oral traditions about their own experience and their own attempt to proclaim the good news.

---

[2] Mohammed (570-632) received visions at Mt. Hira, which led to the Koran, the written source for Islam. Mohammed did not look on Islam as a new religion, but only a return to the original teachings of Moses, other prophets and Jesus.

We find in the New Testament a gradual reference to groups of Jews who would not accept Christ. Not only the Scribes and Pharisees reject Christ and argue with Him but also the Jews in general. Particularly in the brilliant Gospel of John we find frequent reference to the "Jews" turning away from the message and becoming a threat to Jesus. In John V. Jesus cures a sick man at the pool of Bethsaida and "the Jews" are upset because he performed a miracle on a Saturday. When Jesus tried to explain his message we read "But that only made the Jews even more intent on killing him, because, not content with breaking the Sabbath, he spoke of God as his own Father, and so made himself God's equal." In chapter seven of John we read, "No one spoke openly of him, for fear of the Jews." 7:12.

These frequent references to "the Jews," particularly in John can be instrumental in gradually inculcating, among hearers and readers, an unconscious hatred or ill feeling for Jews.

According to Rosemary Ruether, this attitude towards the Jews, fostered by the New Testament and found for many years in the Good Friday Liturgy, helped make Hitler's Holocaust possible, the final culmination of years of Christian oppression, pogroms, expulsions and massacres.

In the Good Friday Liturgy Catholics prayed for "the perfidious Jews." This prayer was the only one of ten when the congregation was not invited also to kneel and pray silently. Inculcating prejudice and bigotry in the official prayer of the church is indeed *outrageous* and it took good Pope John XXIII to finally purge this reprehensible "prayer."

It is time for the church to examine all of its teaching, what it has said, done and acted on through the ages and to confess its guilt wherever it has encouraged hatred, bigotry, and diminution of human and civil rights.

It took the Church over four hundred years to admit it was wrong about Galileo. It is good modeling for parents, teachers and other authority figures, to admit when they are wrong: admit it, ask for forgiveness and move on.

It is time for the church to quit hiding behind a facade of righteousness. The Church is at last coming to terms about child abuse and the sexual exploitation of women.

The Bible was rewritten and edited many times. It was copied, changed, added to. It is time to expunge all subversive reference to "the Jews" in the scriptures. How about using "some people" instead?

CHAPTER 2

HOW THE EARLY CHURCH HANDLED HERESY AND DEVIANTS

The early Christian Church had a hard time getting started. It met with opposition from the Jews who refused to accept Jesus as the messiah or risen Lord. The Romans initially ignored them but gradually turned to persecution because the Christians refused to worship the emperor.

Then to there were various current philosophies that seemed to run counter to the Christian message. These schools of philosophy often posed a threat to Christianity. Indeed they were a threat and we shall see how the ideas of some philosophers permeated and influenced Christian teaching.

The Church had trouble not only from outside, but also frequently from within the ranks of believers. They found dissent, deviation, and possibly heresy. The spoken and written word often takes its meaning from the hearer and the reader. The author's original intent is sometimes misunderstood, twisted, or mistranslated by another. Married persons, employees and employers, voters and politicians, can all attest to being "misunderstood." Commentators spend hours on TV telling the people what some message means. What it actually, "really" means.

Early Christians became confused about salvation, God's nature, Christ's structure, biblical books, the second coming of Christ, morality, celibacy versus marriage, carnal pleasure, the list goes on and on. That list added confusion, through the centuries about baptism, the Eucharist, priesthood, abortion, birth control and a host of other subjects which make it appear that confusion and dissent are part of the program.

The trouble is who is right? William Blake the poet said, "Both read the Bible day and night; but you read black where I read white." Not only is it a question about who is right but how do you handle the person who is wrong? Does error have any rights? What is error and how seriously should it be dealt with?

We frequently think that the internal problems and divisions of Christendom are somewhat recent in the history of the Church. We can point to 1054 AD. when the Orthodox Church separated from the Roman Church over a married clergy and the supremacy of the Pope. We can further list Luther, Calvin, Knox and other reformers from the sixteenth century who began the rupture of Christendom at the time of Protestant Reformation.

Yes, we can, but the elements of dissent and difference have been in the Church from the start and the ways of dealing with it are not new. We have been fighting these battles from the very beginning. We need to know our origins, our history, our pride, arrogance, and mistakes.

Probably the most serious enemies of the human race have been those who thought they possessed the "truth." Certitude leads to closure, defense, attack, bitterness, chagrin, and frequently persecution. Those who do not possess the truth need to be told the truth so they can accept it and get on with their lives.

But what happens if these ignorant souls, after being presented the obvious truth fail to accept it? Must they not, for their own good, be made to see their errant ways to be forced, cajoled ridiculed, punished, and even killed?

This was certainly the mentality of Hitler and we could name an endless list of others, Christians, pagans, Moslems, Jews, Greeks who openly used force to establish their views. Some find it difficult even to accept that there was a holocaust. How could this happen? Many deny clear evidence and say the holocaust never happened. It is difficult to admit that we humans would do such horrible things to one another, that we have done and still do so in the name of truth. In the name of truth, religious truth, people are killed daily in Bosnia, India, Pakistan, the United States, Ireland, everywhere. And all of us who murder, bomb, kill do it for truth. We recently bombed Iraq in cause of "righteousness and humanitarian ethics" over some land that actually belonged to them prior to 1921. We set out to bomb and obliterate one of the oldest civilizations in the world. Why? They are plainly wrong and we are right. We possess the truth.

This attitude was clearly present in the early Church. The Church could have easily been infected with erroneous doctrine and led astray by those who either watered down the doctrine or embellished it by adding to it.

St. Paul indicated to the Galatians "I marvel that you are so quickly deserting him who called you to the grace of Christ, changing to another gospel -- that there are some who trouble you and wish to pervert the gospel of Christ. But even if we or an angel from heaven should preach a gospel to you other than that which we have preached to you, let him be anathema." Gal 1:6-9

Anathema means cursed and excluded from the Kingdom. Strong words and Paul used them seriously. Paul feared that his followers might "fall from a single devotion to Christ." 2Cor11:3 Although Paul no longer felt it was necessary to obey the Old Testament laws, he would allow no deviations or dissent from his teachings.

Paul gets so excited about those who are stirring up the Galatians that he exclaims "Would that those who are unsettling you would mutilate themselves" Gal5:12 He gets carried away and forgets the message of Jesus who preached forgiveness and taking it easy on the ignorant and on sinners. Paul says rather, "If any man does not love the Lord Jesus Christ, let him be anathema." 1Cor 16:22 We can admire Paul's devotion to Christ and the gospel but he seems also to be preaching an attitude that leads to the persecution of dissent itself to and difference of opinion.

Once again we are confronted with the question - does error have any rights? The deeper question is: how can we recognize error and what should we do about it? At the time of Galileo the Church became threatened by the teaching that the earth moved around the sun. This seemed to contradict the Bible and what clearly meets the eye. After all, anyone can see that the sun rises and sets. Actually this is an optical illusion and we now know "for sure" the sun does not rise or set. We still say it does but we know it doesn't.

You can sit in a train waiting for it to depart and when the train alongside of you moves you suffer the illusion that you are moving when you're not. we now know that even solid objects have moving parts inside the molecules. We know that the Hindus are right about Maya, the world of illusion.

Yet when it comes to religion we still preach certitude. Myths are what other people believe. Truths are what we believe. We all need some basic beliefs to live by, some ground for our being and Jesus certainly provided such beliefs. He taught that his disciples were to be known by "love for another." Also the final test for entrance to the Kingdom was how you treated your fellow -- man and woman. "Come, blessed of my Father, to be in possession of the Kingdom prepared for you from the foundation of the world; for I was hungry and you gave me to eat; I was thirsty and you gave me to drink; I was a stranger and you took me in; naked and you covered me; sick and you visited me; I was in prison and you came to me." Mt 25:34

Of course the words of Jesus as quoted above were probably written after many of Paul's letters but perhaps they do emphasize exactly where the stress should be. After all Paul also pointed out charity as the more excellent way, without which all else is but "sounding brass and a clanging cymbal." 1Cor 13:1

Our present world is a dangerous one, not only because of the weapons of destruction that we possess but also because of intolerance, bigotry, and certitude. We have inherited this certitude from the very sources of our Christian beliefs. They help strengthen and encourage us. They also solidify us in our beliefs and help us turn a deaf ear to others. We need to listen. "Faith comes through hearing." Rom 10:17

The most serious problem in the early Church was whether Christians had to obey the Jewish Law. This dispute is treated at great length in Romans, Galatians, and 1Corinthians. Finally a council was held in Jerusalem and this council is outlined in Acts 15:1-35. It is also referred to in Galatians 2:11. Here Paul says he "withstood Peter to his face."

This does present a good way to handle conflict about dogma and morality. People need to get together, exchange ideas and data and reach conclusions. Calling names, persecuting, killing, exiling, enslaving, and excommunicating seem to be not only less noble ways to proceed but also one against the teaching of Jesus, that calls for mercy on the ignorant for forgiveness and for a spirit of humility. "I am among you as one who serves." Jn 13:15

From the time of the Council of Jerusalem to 317 C.E. the Church was on the run, being persecuted everywhere, rejected by the Jews and internally dealing with heresies of all kinds. Gnosticism, which dealt with the mystical approach to Christianity based on quality and separation, finally seemed to die off. Actually many of its ideas about the evils of the flesh, the world, and the necessity for extreme self-denial were incorporated into Christianity through St. Augustine, the teaching of the superiority of celibacy and virginity over marriage and to the rise of hermits and monasticism.

The most serious heresy seemed to center around the nature and personhood of Jesus. How was it possible for Him to be God and Man? It took centuries to work this out by saying he was one person who possessed two natures, the Divine that he shared with the Father and Holy Spirit, and the human he received from Mary.

Arius, around 310 AD., taught that Jesus was the first born of the Father, through whom all was created, the greatest of all, but not quite God. So great was the attraction of Arius and his teaching that the Emperor Constantine, trying to maintain order in his empire, decided to call a Council at Nicea to settle the issue.

Here we have an example of a civil ruler, who for years persecuted the Church, and became deeply involved. He did not like dissension and his clergy fighting and teaching the faithful different doctrines.

From the Council of Nicea 325 C.E. came the famous Nicene Creed, still recited by many Christian believers as a sign of orthodoxy. Arianism did not die out immediately and many forms of it have lasted through the centuries. Some Arian believers were absorbed into the greater church even centuries later.

The word heresy means to pick and choose. Those who regard themselves as correct call those who are not correct heretics. How does one determine who is correct? This problem has afflicted the Church from the beginning and the Church gradually developed a creed, a code of morality and a cult. All religions develop these three areas. Along with these basics came chief teachers, priests, ministers, scriptures, laws, books, interpretations, and finally, punishment.

In the early Church a gradual hierarchy came into being: bishops, priests, deacons. They were all ordained. Jesus ordained no one. He commissioned them. To be a Christian you had to be united with the Bishop, follow his teachings and accept his rules and clergy.

What concerns us here is dissent. The early Christians were dissenters and they were persecuted by many of the Jews and Romans. They represented a threat to established religions and to the proper governing of the empire.

It took about three hundred years and the Christians got the upper hand. Constantine became a Christian and began to push Christianity. In 384 C.E., the Emperor Theodosius made Chrisianity the official State religion. This union of the Church and State led to the glorious vision of the Holy Roman Empire and the Holy Roman Emperor.

This looked like a good thing. The Church and the State seemed to be working together, but it never worked and probably never could. As the Church ceases to be a spiritual force and model and becomes an institution, governed by bureaucrats, it cannot maintain its equilibrium.

The basic question for the Church is "what are you trying to do?" No one objects to Mother Theresa waiting on the poor lepers of India. When she tries to fight for laws against contraception and abortion numerous adversaries arise. This it is when any single person or group of persons tries to impose ideas on others in the name of God, righteousness, whatever.

These sorts of ideas, smoldering for centuries in Bosnia and greater Yugoslavia, to mention an obvious site, erupt and lead to death and destruction, leaving thousands of victims asking why? Some might say, "In the name of truth, we kill mutilate, destroy, rape you. Accept it. It is the law."

When we see these things happen again and again we need to ask ourselves why. How can we stop it? Do we all need to be so adamant about possessing the truth? Even God's truth? Even our understanding of God's truth? Pontius Pilate's question is still a good one, "What is truth?" JU 18:38

CHAPTER 3

PREJUDICE TOWARDS MARRIAGE

(AS TAUGHT BY JEROME, AUGUSTINE, ORIGEN, POPES)

If Jesus founded a Church based on strict doctrine there is no indication from him that marriage is an inferior vocation, less praiseworthy than virginity or celibacy.

A case can be made for the conception of Jesus, that it happened in an extraordinary manner, without sexual intercourse. This same type of conception is found among Greek mythologies or in the story of the conception of Buddha. These stories of miraculous, different types of conception say nothing about marriage being a higher or lower state.

How then did this theology develop? To some extent it came about from the conflict the early Church had with Gnosticism[3] and

---

[3] Gnosticism: means knowledge. Taught the superiority of contemplation, despised the world of matter, stressed secret codes, rules and limited Christianity to a select few. The lingering effects of Gnosticism continue to plague present Christianity.

Manicheanism.[4] Some of it resulted from the emphasis on the Second Coming of Christ. The early Christians waited every Saturday night for the Second Coming of Jesus, the parousia. There were indications in the Gospel stories that the return of "the Son of Man" was imminent.

If this were so, and the frequent discussions lead Paul to write two letters to the Thessalonians on that subject, then why bother getting married and raising a family? Why not just wait in a state of prayer made easier by the absence of family life disturbances?

There has always been a problem in trying to explain the existence of evil. How can a just, wise, all-powerful, all knowing God allow evil? This problem is addressed at great length in the book of Job and no answer is given. Jesus said the heavenly Father allows the life-giving rain to fall on the just and the unjust. Out of Persia came another answer, from Zoroaster. There are two Gods, one creates good and the other evil.

The evil God creates is not only trouble, death, and destruction, but also the material world and the world of pleasure. Gnosticism sprang from these roots and it taught that only the highest quality spiritual life was acceptable. Matters of the body like pleasure -- are totally unacceptable. Before his conversion Augustine was a Manichaean and many of their ideas taint the thinking and writing of Augustine.

In their efforts to ward off the threat of Manicheanism and Gnosticism the early Fathers of the Church took to the pulpit and the pen. The Gnostics said that since the body was evil Christ never even became man in the flesh. He only "appeared" to be fully human.

The Fathers of the church wanted to protect the key doctrine of the Incarnation so they began a frontal attack on Gnosticism. As happens frequently when a conquering nation settles among the conquered they not only impose their culture but they accept some of the conquered culture. They adjust to it, absorb it.

---

[4] Manicheanism: Mani, a follower of Zoroaster, was crucified in Persia in 276 CE. His explanation of the problem of evil and negative forces led to the positing of two Gods, one of good, the other of evil. This teaching still exists among Christians who attribute super human power to evil spirits. Of course the survival of the human species depends how we answer the question: whose side are you on? The question for many is: where is righteousness?

Thus we find a certain hatred of the body creeping into early Christian literature. Earlier Paul in 1Corintheans 9:4,5 asserted his right to eat and drink and take a wife with on his journeys as did the other apostles and Cephas (Peter). It is asserted clearly in 1Timothy 3:2 and Titus 1:6 that bishops were expected to be married, but only once.

By the time of Origen, an opponent of Gnosticism, the superiority of virginity had reached such heights that Origen even castrated himself to show his devotion to the concept. Origen had apparently been taken in by some of the ideas of the very people with whom he was in conflict. Although Origen is looked upon as one of the most learned men in the early Church, his reputation was tainted by his act of self-mutilation. Origen also taught that it was wrong to approach the sanctuary of Church for Holy Communion if a person had sex during the previous twenty-four hours.

The teachings of Origen were continued by St. Jerome, who translated the Bible into Latin from the Greek and Hebrew. This version, the Vulgate was used by many translators seeking an English version. Some of the books of the Vulgate, from the Alexandrian Canon are not used in some translations and are regarded as apocrypha.

Although Jerome spent most of his life living off the estates of women, like the widow Paula, and staying in proximity to them in adjoining quarters, Jerome seemed to be firmly against sex and held marriage in low esteem. Jerome railed particularly against Jovinian a contemporary adversary who taught that marriage and eating and drinking were equal to celibacy and fasting. Jerome convinced his friend Pop Damasus into excommunicating Jovinian. Pope Damasus was really upset that any priest would think of having sex after ordination. He said those who did, cast "shame on honorable religion." It is a "crime", they are "masters of sin, enslaved to lust." This same abhorrence of sex and conflicts between clerical and married life occupied a great deal of the attention in the letters and writings of Pope Siricius.

This tradition of animosity for marriage and sex was brought to a head by St. Augustine, the most unexpected source. He was extremely worldly, and had an illegitimate son by his concubine. His mother Monica never tired of remonstrating him and praying for his conversion. While in Milan, teaching rhetoric, Augustine came under the influence of Ambrose, a bishop and lawyer, a severe man.

He suddenly was inspired to read the Scriptures and the passage he chose randomly advised him that "salvation came, not from wantonness and drunkenness, but by putting on the Lord Jesus." He took instructions from Ambrose, sent his concubine and son back to Africa and was baptized. He would be prosecuted for desertion today.

After studying theology and the Scriptures he was ordained and eventually became the Bishop of Hippo in North Africa. He ordered all his priests into a monastery and began to enforce celibacy.

Augustine developed a hatred of sex and pleasure and began to systematize the cumulative teaching on marriage and sex into a unified approach. He linked original sin to sexual intercourse and he became obsessed with the dangers of sex. This total and enveloping mania not only influenced the writings of Augustine but has held Christianity in a vise ever since.

The church, from the time of Augustine cannot seem to shake itself of this obsession and its truly criminal attitude toward marriage, sexual intercourse and anything related to it. The Church's moral theology devotes greater sections to sins of sex than to any other kind. The Church, from Augustine on, has been in a full court press against marriage and bodily pleasure.

According to Genesis and Jesus' teaching, marriage and sex are blessed by God and is not only totally legitimate but recommended. But reading The Confessions of St. Augustine and his The City of God we reach the conclusion that sex is dangerous. In the sections devoted to commentary on sex Augustine seems to single out women as the purveyors of this wanton life.

It seems that this pernicious teaching has reverberations in other areas of theology such as redemption, salvation, and Mariology.[5] If sex is so bad Mary certainly conceived Jesus without sex, had no other children, remained a perpetual virgin.

It is difficult to see how a theologian can take a natural act, shared by the animal world, and lower levels of creation, if there is such a level, and turn it into something sinful, lascivious, and able to keep people away from Holy Communion at the Lord's Supper.

---

[5] A branch of theology, the study of God, Christ and the sacraments which covers material related to the mother of Jesus as to her being the mother of God and her special prerogative.

One can observe here a definite restriction of human rights that has affected humankind to this day. To get to where we are going we need to know our starting point, how far off we have veered, and then set our sights straight before proceeding to the "fullness" St. Paul speaks of.

In the next section we will see how celibacy came to be a "law" in the western part of Christendom. It came out of unfounded assumptions or erroneous thinking and it basically curtails human rights. This is our focus throughout this discussion: human and civil rights.

CHAPTER 4

THE IMPOSITION OF CELIBACY

(AN INFRINGEMENT ON HUMAN RIGHTS)

Sexuality is part of being human. In the world of animals there are males and females and there seems to be a drive of nature to mate. This mating insures the continuance of the species and so the sex drive is produced by nature to guarantee that humans and plants and animals will always be on earth.

Somehow, different types of mating seasons and even places developed. Salmon swim upstream at incredible odds to mate. Elephants mate only every two years. Some animals stay mates for life. Some have elaborate rituals. The variety and splendor is infinite, rich, spontaneous and unstoppable.

Yet somehow the Catholic Church has imposed celibacy on its clergy. Why? There is no good answer to this question, either based on nature or on theology.

Christianity stems from Judaism and the roots there say that children are important. Fertility is a blessing and sexuality is important in human relations.

So what happened? As far as we know Jesus never married since there are no references to his wife. Yet Jesus had many women followers, some of them like Mary Magdalene were his special friends.

These women followed Jesus as he went about, even to his death and resurrection. Jesus broke taboos to talk to and empower women as he did with the Samaritan woman.

Once again we ask: what happened? The early Church, and especially St. Paul were caught up in the second coming of Christ, which was supposed to happen any minute. In such a case why bother to marry, settle down and raise a family? Time is almost ending and the business at hand is salvation, preaching the gospel and preparing for the return of Jesus. This was Paul's message. Read his earliest writing in 1 and 2 Thessalonians.

Along with this were other teachings with which the Church had tangled and had conquered, but apparently not without absorbing some of their influence. This was the teaching of Manicheanism and Gnosticism. These early heresies taught that matter was evil and therefore they linked sexual intercourse to evil, since intercourse was in and through the flesh. Besides, it extended the problem by producing more humans, prone to evil and materialism.

Thus Paul, Augustine, and Pope Sericius all jumped on the bandwagon and agreed that marriage was a vocation inferior to virginity and celibacy. Jesus never imposed such rigidity or what we might now call stupidity. To think that an all wise God would make such a creature that had to propagate itself through sex and then say that the very act is possibly evil or at least demeaning and needs to be shunned is actually unthinkable and arrogant.

Celibacy came out of hatred of sex, fear and hatred of women. The fact that it has such an unsavory origin and is UN-Christian in its roots would seem to make it suspect, undesirable and something to get rid of. Still today the Church, at least the Vatican where *official*

Christendom reigns, still exalts virginity and celibacy over marriage and still insists that its clergy be celibate.

Celibacy did not become a law in the western Church until the Second Lateran Council of 1139. Even then many clergy paid little attention to it because they could still marry clandestinely. This possibility was not dealt with until the Council of Trent (1545 - 1563) ruled that all marriages to be valid must be contracted in the presence of a priest and two witnesses. After that point, legal, Church approved marriage became impossible canonically for western clergy.

The Church was able to impose this "law of celibacy" on all clergy because the Church has the power to bind and loose. After all if you want to be a cleric, you must choose to give up sex and marriage. This means basically that you must cease to be human, at least in this important aspect of humanness.

The Church is very heavy on the "natural law," a subject we will deal with later. Yet the Church seems openly to contradict itself in this case, ordering its clergy to put aside the urges of nature, to stifle the hormones and to give up sex.

There is no good scriptural or theologically deduced reason for virginity or celibacy. Not only is there no good reason, it seems to create the opposite of sanctity and holiness. It puts priests in the bad position of devoting all their time and energy to such spiritual quests when they cannot possibly remain on such a course as evidenced by the many who do not.

Celibacy was practiced in the early Church mostly by monks who withdrew from the "world" and lived a communal life in monasteries. Here they fasted from meats to weaken the sexual urge, worked hard physically in the fields and barns, spent long hours in group and private prayer. They sleep inadequately so they were tired most of the time. They had little or no contact with women. Is celibacy possible in such an environment? Yes, it was and is, but today's diocesan priests do not live in monasteries in the desert.

They have frequent contact with women and girls. Whenever males and females get together in study, sport, recreation, projects, or any activity, the hormones will kick into action and sexual urges will result. When a man and woman feel these urges they will feel like acting on them. If a man is married and has a wife with whom he can have legitimate sex, he has a way of controlling these desires. The celibate must try to live like a monk in a world that is far from the monastic milieu.

The false attitude that virginity is superior to marriage, the fear and hatred of women and their so-called "seductive" ways has led the Church leaders of the past, its teachers and hierarchy, to impose on its clergy a burden that not only is unbearable but is inhuman and against "human rights."

It would be similar to saying that to live an outstanding life as a member of the church you must become a slave, give yourself over to a master and lose all human dignity. At one time St. Paul and the Church condoned slavery and recommended how slaves and masters could get along. At one time the Church was totally against and forbade usury. The Church can examine data, cultural phenomena, make adjustments, and change.

It is time for the Church to see that marriage, sex, women, and pleasure, are all OK, at least when done according to certain rights, duties, safety precautions, and limitations. We are not okaying child molestation's, rape, and free sex, when we say sex is good in itself and marriage is just as good as virginity. For most people it might be better because it is normal and natural.

It is time for the Church to make celibacy optional for its clergy. No one should be forced to give up human rights to serve God or humanity. They might chose to do this, maybe temporarily. They should not be forced. It is time to take in new, valid information, reexamine antiquated untenable positions, drop them, and get on with tackling the *real* problems of our age: poverty, racism, sexism, war, drugs, crime, rape, and abuse. Why pour energy into a dead-end? Why use energy to restrain a human energy? There is no need and besides its wrong.

CHAPTER 5

THE CHURCH AS A CIVIL POWER

Many people do not know that at one time the Roman Catholic Church was the sole civil ruler of a large segment of middle Italy. According to Christ's words he never intended the Church to be a civil power. "Render unto Caesar the things that are Caesar's and to God the things that are God's".

However, it happened, and initially almost by default, then by decree, then by precedent, the Papal States' came into being. This institution made the Pope the a civil ruler of a large segment of Italy and thereby a valued ally in war or peace. The Pontiff had power, spiritual and temporal. It varied from century to century, from Pope to Pope, but it existed from shortly after the conversion of Constantine in 317 CE until September 20, 1870. It still remains, but no so obviously.

When Constantine, the ruler of the world around 300 CE, decided to move his government to Byzantium in the East, he left an exarch in Ravenna, Italy, to govern in his place. The Romans were used to

Caesar being in Rome, especially if he was not out to war. They expected a presence in town. This was gone when Constantine moved east to establish a city, in his name to be the civil center of the world and of Christendom. He founded the city of Constantine, Constantinople.

Gradually the Pope became the civil ruler of Rome and its environs. He took care of taxes, water supplies, laws, armies, and conflicts. At various times marauders and roaming tribes invaded Italy and the Pope could not fight them off. Sometimes his mere presence did so, as when Pope Leo the Great confronted Attila the Hun and the warrior inexplicably withdrew from Italy in 451 CE.

By the end of the eighth century CE the papal armies were unable to contain invaders. Pepin the Short, Charles Martel and finally Charlemagne conquered them for the Pope and shortly thereafter they reciprocated giving each other honors. The Pope solemnly crowned Charlemagne King of the Holy Roman Empire and Charlemagne formally declared the Pope the Civil Ruler of central Italy. Byzantium no longer had any claim over it. This, with other differences, led to the fracture of the eastern from the western church in 1054 CE.

So, from 325 CE to 1870 CE, the Pope was the civil ruler of Rome and its environs. At times these lands were taken away, divided, and contested, but no one seemed to think they didn't really belong to the papacy. This historical occurrence became an unhappy burden for the papacy, a lumbering albatross around its neck.

Yet when Rome and the Papal States were seized by Garibaldi and the "red shirt" brigade, the Pope and many Catholics were shocked, chagrined and mortified. The Pope himself fled for safety. Actually, they were not after him but after the land! a movement was afoot to unify Italy and Garibaldi and his followers finally had enough nerve to say that Italy belonged to the Italians and the only way to unite the northern and southern sections of Italy was to seize the Papal States.

They left the Pope alone in Vatican City where the Pope referred to himself as "the Prisoner of the Vatican." This problem was finally solved, by, of all people, Mussolini. Pope Puis XI and Mussolini agreed through the Lateran Pacts of 1929 that Vatican City, with its 108.7 acres of land, plus the Papal summer palace would be a sovereign state, fully independent. Italy also gave the papacy a large cash settlement for the rest of the land.

The Papacy still functions as a Church and a civil power, since it maintains embassies around the world and receives heads of states as a head of state. The papacy is very involved in politics in Italy, the United States, Poland, Central and South America. It watches laws carefully, especially laws about birth control, abortion, and marriage.

The Church will excommunicate persons from the sacraments if necessary to make sure they do not civilly get out of line. Recently the Bishop of Lincoln, Nebraska ex-communicated Catholics for belonging to certain organizations.

The Church exerted not only spiritual power in terms of salvation and forgiveness of sin but also wielded great civil power at various times throughout its history. When we come to the Crusades and the Inquisition we will see more specific examples of the Church reaching into areas of civil rights and doing quite naturally.

Because the Church fostered buildings and the expression of art about the mysteries of Christianity one also finds the Church as a so-called civil patron of the arts. The Church provided not only the mysteries, stories and persons for artists to depict, but also provided the money, the jobs, the continuity.

Pope Julius II who fought long, hard wars at the head of papal armies to regain lands lost during the dissolute reign of his predecessor, Alexander VI, was also a patron of the arts and personally commandeered Michelangelo to work at the Vatican. He felt, that since he was pope, he had charge not only of armies and spiritual affairs (to which he paid little attention) but also of what artists did, where and how they did it. The concept of the union of Church and State has been a romantic ideal since Augustine broached the subject in the *City of God*. The idea was that we are all temporarily here to work out our salvation and the best way to achieve this is for the spiritual and temporal to work together, hand-in- hand. This would be a true union of Church and State. After all, if the church has the guiding principles of eternal truth and light why shouldn't the state be guided by these principles and so aid the Church in achieving its goals?

This same concept is used by those who embrace Islamic Fundamentalism and Jewish Orthodoxy, Hinduism, and many other religions. They think they are right so why shouldn't their principles lead and guide the State? After all, it's for the benefit of humanity. This is now (1996) happening for instance in Afghanistan.

So we see that the concept of the Church as a civil power has far reaching consequences. The Protestants of Northern Ireland want the English Crown to "protect" them from Catholics. American Catholics ally themselves with Fundamentalists to get certain laws passed and to keep others from getting passed. In these and thousands of cases world-wide, there is a seeking for a "union of Church and State." In 1996 in the United States, certain fundamental groups are trying tooth and nail to control the U.S. government so they can enforce "Christian values".

Such a concept has never worked for the benefit of the whole. It never protects the dissidents, the minorities, those of differing opinions. Those who hold the reigns of power do not believe that ignorance, evil, stupidity or falsehood has any right.

The history of the Church as a civil power has been a long recitation of blocking human civil rights. Being a civil power only makes this happen more quickly and thoughtlessly. The loss of the Papal States has been a benefit to humanity and the Church.

CHAPTER 6

THE CRUSADES

AN ABUSE OF CIVIL RIGHTS

Usually when some great social event takes place, numerous causes and trends are discernible. When the Crusades began at the end of the eleventh century we might wonder what brought about this bizarre event. War is always a disaster, but after one is over the description of the catastrophe bears little resemblance to what actually took place. What is written is epic history. We retell it to our advantage and make it look glorious.

I remember seeing the movies of World War II. They portrayed the fever and fervor in the land and the songs were exciting. "We're coming over and we won't be back till it's over, over there." The movies showed our men planning their strategies and the storming of the beaches. Mostly the enemy was killed but none of our heroes.

We still look at 'our wars' in grandiose manner. The most powerful nation on earth attacks Grenada, Panama, small Iraq, and we celebrate with hoopla, parades, and congratulatory speeches.

The crusades fit in this picture. The Crusades were a stupid idea to start with, ill-conceived, poorly planned, and in some cases, not planned at all. They were a failure, harmful to human rights, and violated the tenets of Christianity. They also violated common sense.

Shortly after the death of Mohammed in 632, Jerusalem and Palestine fell under the domination of Islam. The Muslims, contrary to popular opinion, did not impose Islam on any of the people they conquered. They did impose taxes. They had great respect for the prophets of Judaism and Christianity. They honored Moses and Christ. They had reverence for holy places. Originally Mohammed ordered his followers to pray towards Jerusalem, but when he saw he could not convert many Jews, he changed the direction toward Mecca.

Muslims were not or are not *infidels*. Infidel comes from two Latin words, *in* and *fides*. It literally means *without faith*. Followers of the Koran are hardly people without faith. They believe many of the same things Jews and Christians believe. They worship the same God, referred to as Allah in Arabic. They believe in prayer, penance, and the moral law. They are definitely not *infidels*!

Moreover, the Muslims believed in keeping the Sacred places open for worship and visitation by Jews and Christians. The idea that the Christians were hindered from seeing these places is preposterous.

The Byzantine Emperor Alexuis Comnenus had tried to regain the land of Palestine for his rule but failed. These lands, still being fought over and argued about today, were important areas that connected with other more important places. They were linked with Egypt, Syria, Iraq, Persia, and Turkey. They were part of international trade routes. Plus they contained "holy places" and shrines.

The Emperor appealed to Pope Urban II for help. It was while Urban II was in France at Clermont that the idea of a crusade overcame him. Urban II was trying to prevent warring factions and emerging nations from spending their time killing one another. He had proclaimed The Truce of God and then the brilliant idea occurred to him to give the warriors and knights something to do. After all, this was the age of chivalry.

Supposedly, at the Council of Clermont, Urban addressed a large throng of bishops, noblemen, and people. They were roused to excitement when Urban called for a "holy war" to regain the holy lands. According to reports, they explained, almost in unison, "God wills it." As if the God who prohibited killing and recommended love had a revoked his earlier command and now recommended mass murder, for that was what happened.

It is true that the Seljuk Turks had gained control over Jerusalem and Bethlehem and had committed atrocious hostilities not only on the Christians they conquered, but also on their own Moslems. Peter the Hermit began preaching the concept of a crusade and Urban II finally bought it. It was 1095 when this ill-fated decision was made.

The Crusade was to begin August 15, 1096. An admirable time, since it was the feast of the Assumption of the Blessed Virgin Mary into heaven. Not only did God will it but also His Mother. The knights wore the cross of Christ on their chests and fought in chivalry for Mary.

The Pope, to encourage more participation, promised an indulgence[6] of freedom from punishment for sins already forgiven, and guaranteed salvation for anyone who died in the quest. This promise is not unlike one found in the Koran that speaks of Jihad, the holy war, and instant paradise for those who die for it.

No king took part in this first crusade but as they marched through many regions on their way, a motley and totally disorganized gang, robbed and plundered as they encountered many people who did not meet their definition of "Christian." If they weren't Christian they deserved to be pillaged and killed. If they were Christian and didn't cooperate they also were subjected to punishment.

Hans Mayer writes, "Inflamed by irresponsible preachers and attracted by the wealth of the important Jewish communities on the Rhineland, they indulged themselves in pogroms on a scale hitherto unprecedented in the Middle Ages."

---

[6] The concept developed that even after sins were forgiven a residue of punishment remained, referred to as temporal punishment due for sins. This residue could be atoned for by prayers, good works, fasting etc. In this case going on a crusade gained an indulgence. At the time of Luther the Pope said those contributing to rebuilding St. Peters could receive an indulgence.

Each crusade brought it's own type of death, plunder and destruction. It would be impossible to believe that a Children's Crusade could take place as it did in 1212. All the children either perished from disease or famine or were captured and taken into slavery. That an adult population would allow such a catastrophe, under the sponsorship of the Church, is unthinkable. Yet it happened.

The Crusaders expected to be maintained by local populations as they moved across Europe, the Balkans, and Asia Minor. If they weren't received well they proceeded to kill resistors and to take their food supplies. Many crusading parties camped in Constantinople, almost permanently, and expected to be fed and kept warm.

In 1204 a group of Crusaders, under the direction of Genoese merchants, practically destroyed Constantinople. These acts made the schism with the Orthodox church that formally took place in 1054, frozen in stone and almost irrevocable. This break continues to the present time.

It took the first group of Crusaders three years to reach and conquer Jerusalem. By the time they achieved this goal they were mad with the untamed excitement of religious fever. The intoxication of victory, coupled with religious fanaticism burst forth into a blood-bath of all the inhabitants of Jerusalem. It was said that "they waded ankle-deep in blood, through streets covered with bodies."

These act of violence intensified the conflicts between Jews and Christians and Moslems and Christians. These animosities, committed particularly by Moslems and Christians, towards each other and against the Jews separately continued to this day all over the world, seen presently in the Middle East and Bosnia.

The Crusades have been glorified in literature and the image of gallant knights and kings linger in our imaginations. The tale of Robin Hood is intertwined with the tale of King Richard the Lionhearted, off on a crusade, captured and returning magnificently.

With the blessing of many Popes and illustrious saints like Bernard of Clairvoux and King Louis IX of France, the Crusades seemed to exhibit a renewal of Christendom and religious fever, unmatched since the beginnings of the Church and during the ages of the martyrs.

Yet, what the Crusades were in reality turned out to be a catastrophe. The Crusades, in their idea of regaining the holy lands, ultimately failed. Whatever sections they regained, they ultimately lost. In their wake they left death, destruction, rape, plunder, and ill-will. The crusaders, by and large, totally ignored any civil rights, or any other kinds of rights of others. They almost felt it was their prerogative to inflict atrocities on others, and then not only to be forgiven, but even to be rewarded.

The conviction that one possesses the truth can be dangerous for others who may not possess that truth or ever want to accept it when offered. Many have died in the name of Christ. We shall continue on this as we move on to the Inquisition and Reformation. In shame, the Church and members often are not seen on the side of the poor and the helpless, nor friendly toward non-believers.

CHAPTER 7

THE INQUISITION

(A WORD THAT STILL STRIKES TERROR IN OUR HEARTS)

The Inquisition was a medieval ecclesiastical tribunal for the preservation of faith, and was instituted by Pope Gregory IX (1222-41). It had a three fold purpose: first, to enquire (Enquire: hence Inquisition) into the spread of doctrines opposed to faith (heresies); second, to call before tribunals all suspected of heresy; and third, to punish their infidelity, to convince them of error and to exhort them to Penance.

Earlier the Second Lateran Council in 1139 had ordered civil rulers to combat heresy with imprisonment, confiscation of personal and real property, and death. From the beginning of the Inquisition, Church and State functioned together on these issues as a team.

Frequently a kind of fair was held, called "auto de fe" which was really a meeting about the faith. At the auto de fe, heretics were publicly tried on a platform occupied by clerics and inquisitors and, if found guilty, were transferred to another platform where civil rulers presided and administered the punishments handed out by the Inquisitors.

This institution lead to the condemnation of many innocent people who were presumed guilty if charged. There was no way to defend yourself. A lack of confession led to torture, imprisonment and starvation. If you confessed you died or were tortured and imprisoned.

The Inquisition never got any milder, it only got worse. Ultimately it led to the merciless pursuit of so-called witches and midwives, thought to possess the power of sorcery, purchased from the devil himself.

Witchery was always thought to point to demonic possession, heresy and an outright defection from God. Women who had learned home-spun truths about medicine and the use of herbs, exotic mixtures that often healed were deemed to be witches, became suspect, singled out for trial, and eventually burned at the stake.

This type of thinking, that anything unusual, especially if done by a woman, was automatically questioned and needed close scrutiny, led to the ultimate murder of such a successful figure as Joan of Arc. After all, how could the English be beaten by a woman anyway, and how bewitched were the French that they let her do it? Her own people betrayed her, ungrateful for her magnificent service, and the English burned her as a witch and heretic. The Church watched and only later canonized her a saint. She was a victim of the Inquisition.

Before we tell more about the Inquisition and witches, let us examine how such an institution got started. What nurtured it? How was it possible? Hitler had his origins in the culture that made him possible. So it was and is with the Church.

If we want to find the causes of the Inquisition we will need to look at the institutional Church at the time of origin. The Church not only began the Inquisition itself in a formal manner, but also caused it by setting up a culture that would lead to it and then fed it until it wore out and died. And, although it died formally, its remnants remain as do many of its practices. The Catholic Church today has put this type of treatment on the purveyors of "liberation theology".

The Church went from an early stage of being persecuted, to becoming the official Church of the Roman Empire. It went from poverty to riches in a few hundred years. The Church began to acquire property, to build cathedrals and castles, to erect huge monasteries and convents and to rule over tax free farm lands and cattle. It became profitable to be a priest and a bishop.

There were very few prestigious jobs available in those days, say from the beginning of the Church in 35 A.D., up to the time before the industrial revolution. Many found the Church a good place to gain a high position and most noble families selected one or more of their sons to be priests and bishops.

The Papacy itself was often controlled by one or another of Italian families, like the Borgias or Farneses, the Medici, or by a king in Italy or elsewhere. Many bishops held more than one see and frequently purchased them from Rome. If you wanted to live a life of luxury, ease, and sensuality, you could find no better way to do it than to join the clergy. Often no study was required and you could even acquire an episcopal palace while still a youth, if the Pope so appointed.

Celibacy began formally in 1179 but was not enforced until the Council of Trent (1545-1563). So you could be a priest or bishop and have mistresses and hardly anyone objected. The formal Church mostly fell into a pursuit of sensuality, greed, and total neglect of spirituality.

Yet, there were individuals and groups who knew this lifestyle wasn't right and caused neglect of the Church's mission. They began to foment and demand reform. Many founded select spiritual societies and groups. They reacted against the materialism of the Church and sometimes went so far in the other direction that they fell into heresy. Of course, those in high places, who neglected spiritual pursuits could easily recognize dogmatic and moral error.

The dualistic influence of Zoroaster,[7] the Gnostics, the Manicheans never completely left the Church. Now it surged forth under the impetus of the Waldensians,[8] and the Albigentians,[9] also

---

[7] Founder of a popular religion in Persia. Mani, a disciple of Zoroaster had great influence also on Christianity. Many Christian teachings can be traced to their writings.

[8] Waldensians; followers of Peter Waldo from Lyons, France. Waldo taught poverty the evils of war. Since his adherents were untrained and rejected sinful priests they were soon persecuted by the Inquisition.

called Cathari (the pure). These groups basically taught that material things, the body, sex, and marriage, were evil along with eating meat and imbibing strong drink. They practiced severe penance, wore frugal clothes and taught the value of poverty.

They were so much different from the average Christian that they were easily identified and then called heretics. Inquisitors were told that finding a spirit of poverty, abjectness, humility and kindness were almost sure signs of heresy. To what depths had the Church fallen that this were true! Maybe today the same is said of the poor who "deserve what befalls them".

The Popes and Bishops and lower clergy were alarmed at this ruse of heresy and developed the Inquisition to root it out. To have such a process a group, absolutely certain it possesses the truth is needed as well as another group who seems to be deviating from truth. A body of doctrine, covering dogma and morals, had developed since the time of Christ and was formally held and taught as "official."

Many of these teachings were found in the writings of the Fathers of the Church like Jerome and Augustine. During the Middle Ages these were taught in universities as in Paris by men like Albert the Great and by his chief disciple, Thomas Aquinas who finally summarized all of Catholic doctrine in the Summa Theological (1276). Thomas Aquinas, known as the angelic doctor became the luminary whom the Church turned to and still does. To deviate from his teachings has made one suspect even to this day.

Although many of his teachings are plainly wrong and Thomas Aquinas had some peculiar ideas about sex, he did not think it evil. It was also said that priests and bishops who were living in six could not validly make or give the Sacraments. This would have been a real problem for the church so it was impelled to attack. And attack it did!

At first the Inquisition was entrusted to local Bishops and civil rulers but frequently they lacked the will to continue this relentless pursuit. It *was* like a virus in the Church bringing destruction and death that would not go away. Some Bishops and preachers were obsessed

---

[9] Albigentians: numerous in the town of Albi in southern France. Rejected the Old Testament since they claimed it came from the evil God posited by the Manichaeans. They branded sex as utterly evil. There practically wiped out by a crusade instigated by Pope Innocent III.

with idea of rooting out heresy and witchcraft and nothing could stop them.

Two Dominican preachers, Henry Institoris and James Sprenger, convinced Pope Innocent VIII to publish his so-called Witches' Bull which outlined the evils of witchcraft and the appointment of Institoris and Sprenger as Inquisitors about this problem.

The Pope was so sure he was right that he proclaimed, "If any man dare to impinge the pages of our declaration --- let him know he incurs the wrath of Almighty God and of the Blessed Apostles Peter and Paul."

Institoris and Sprenger were also so self-assured that they published in 1486 their infamous treaty *Malleus Maleficarum,* the Hammer of the Witches. In it they outlined the evils of witchcraft and how it must be rooted out. They said witchery originates in carnal lust, insatiable in certain women. They indicated that some of these witches had had sex with devils and derived their extraordinary power from the evil one.

This madness was still infecting the Church in 1623 when Gregory XV railed against women who had pacts with the devil, used black magic and caused death. Gregory advised that all such so women should be turned over to civil authorities for execution.

In the United States we have witnessed this madness in the Church when the Salem witch hunts and trials took place, under the direction of the rigid Puritan and Protestant Church. Witch-hunting is not endemic to any particular Church. It seems to be the result of certitude that I possess the truth and you do not thus you need only to be sought out, persecuted and even killed, but rightfully, for your own good and for the good of the community you must be purged. After all, error has no rights. It has no rights in science, math, grammar or religion. All these domains protect their own "truths".

There is mention of witchcraft in the Bible. Exodus 22:48 says, *"thou shalt not suffer a sorceress to live."* In Deuteronomy God cautions the Israelites to watch out for anyone who uses divination or who are enchanters, sorcerers, or wizards. St. Paul in Galatians 5:19-20 advises recent converts beware of idolatry and socery. The definitions of sorcerers or witches were never clearly given so it was left to interpretation and application. This frequently results in aberrations far from the intent of the speaker.

If Christ *said "the gates of hell shall never prevail against the Church,"* why is there all this anxiety about rooting out falsehood and bad practices? Pope John Paul II in his recent encyclical letter *Splendor Veritatis* seems bent on extricating false teachings, once again, mostly about sex. He is intent on exposing error - the opposite of what he teaches -- truth.

It is good to be a person of conviction and of principle. However, it is also good to be open, searching and tolerant. Jesus was, and he recommended to his followers *"Do not judge and you shall not be judged."*

The extraordinary power of the Inquisition against civil rights manifested itself clearly in Spain during the reign of Ferdinand and Isabella around 1480. There the Inquisition was aimed not so much at heretics per se but at non-believers.

There were many devout Jews and Moors, Spanish Muslims, who lived throughout Spain. Many of them were prosperous farmers and merchants. The Spanish crown gave them orders to convert to Christianity or flee the country. In many instances when they converted, they were accused of trickery and insincerity and trumped up charges were brought against them so they lost either way.

These practices were overlooked by the official Church and often the Church Inquisitors cooperated. The Church spawned, fostered and fed the horrors of the Inquisition as they did the Crusades. In the name of truth, horrible atrocities were committed.

Many Churches today still fell they possess the truth and only they. This attitude leads to positions like the Inquisition. Today Pope John Paul II says any Catholic University which does not teach everything he says as "truth" should no longer be called a Catholic School. Theologians, moralists and scripture scholars have no rights, only the Pope and bishops have.

The Popes often spurn their own committees if they appeared to disagree, as in the Birth Control Commission. The "official Church" has had numerous theologians expelled and silenced for teaching what was deemed "heresy." In Germany we can point to the renowned Hans Kung and in the United States to Father Joseph Curran, formerly Moral Theology Professor at Catholic University.

The Holy Office, the Congregation of Faith is a direct heir to the Inquisition. Almost all institutional Churches have doctrinal investigative bodies to investigate Bishops with lax ideas on homosexuality.

As St. Bernard said, "The road to hell is paved with good intentions." So, these bodies can frequently expel, expunge, isolate and ultimately, "kill off" these purveyors of what they call error. One would wonder if Christ suddenly appeared at one of their trials if they would feel confident and not be ashamed.

Jesus cautioned "the sons of thunder," James and John not to call for severe punishment on non-believers. He forgave Peter, talked gently to Judas and even encouraged him to do what he had to do. "Blessed are the merciful, the meek, the clean of heart." We like to think that the Inquisition is a thing of the past. Would that this was true. Its spirit reigns in our midst. It kills the human psyche and human bodies.

CHAPTER 8

THE REFORMATION

REDUCTION OF RIGHTS BY CATHOLICS AND PROTESTANTS THE HUGUENOTS

On the eve of All Saints' Day, October 31, 1517, Martin Luther, an ordained priest and Augustinian Monk, posted on the door of the Castle Church his *famous Ninety-Five Theses.*

In these theses Luther attacked the teaching of the Catholic Church on indulgences and how this doctrine was executed. He also said the Pope had no power over purgatory and basically Luther set to put severe limits on Papal teaching and administrative authority. This procedure was a common method of provoking debate and challenging any and all to come forward and take the opposite side.

At this time the Pope was Leo X, a Medici Renaissance man from Florence. He was little interested in Church dogma, doctrine or even morality. Also, he was not skilled in theology. He dealt with Luther in a haphazard, intermittent manner. Because his civil power was largely limited to the Papal States, the center of Italy, he could not control the so-called Holy Roman Emperor nor any of his subjects.

In Germany, nationalism was on the rise. Also, humanism, the pursuit of learning and art encouraged intellectual activity and local rulers were tired of the papacy draining their money for projects in Rome. Now it was the rebuilding of St. Peter's Basilica, the present (1996) existing papal Church. The elector of Saxony, Frederick the Wise, for his own reasons, protected Luther from falling into the hands of the Pope. If the Pope could have gotten a hold of Luther he would have been imprisoned and ultimately executed. There might never have been a "Protestant Reformation."

The term "Protestant" was originated by a Catholic majority at a debate at the Diet of Worms, held to iron out difficulties by Catholics and Lutherans. There seemed to be a lack of will in Germany by civil and religious authority to recognize the danger of these "Protestants". Catholics underestimated the outcome of the teachings and writings of Martin Luther. A giant revolution was taking place that would forever change the answer to the question: What is Christianity?

This revolution would affect the definitions of belief systems that had been in place for 1500 years. They would affect church governance, the doctrine of salvation, the relationship of Church and State, and would cause an earth-shaking emergence of intolerance, death, and destruction that has not diminished to this day.

In the name of "religious truth" Catholics and Protestants are killing one another in Northern Ireland. Orthodox Serbs have killed catholic Croats and Bosnian Muslims. The civil rights of millions of people now living are impugned and persecution continues because of religious beliefs. Christians, both Protestants and Catholics have been guilty of the mass murder of 6,000,000 Jews during World War II.

The Protestant Reformation, while freeing millions to seek the truth for themselves in the scripture, quickly led to certain individuals introducing a new system of rigidity enforced on people in the name of "truth" and "God's will."

Luther did not intend to start a revolt but once it started he was appalled. He did not realize the implications of his ideas. Remember the adage, "When your backyard is full of alligators, don't forget you only intended to drain the swamps."

Luther's ideas were picked up by Zwingli in Geneva and John Calvin in Paris. The invention of printing a century before led to the wide scale publication of the theses and pamphlets of Martin Luther. Luther's ideas of faith alone, the scripture alone and the sovereignty of God alone, were of great interest to Calvin.

The changes also interested King Henry VIII of England, at this time (1522) a devout Catholic. He was unnerved by rumblings from Germany, especially Luther's publication, the *Babylonian Captivity*. Henry had drawn up and signed an attack on Luther's orthodoxy. For this Henry was granted the title, "Defender of the Faith," by the Pope , a title still held, strangely enough by the reigning monarch of England. Henry declared himself Head of Church and separated from Rome in 1535. This new division brought the bloodshed and violence that continues in Northern Ireland to the present.

Luther's ideas probably were very influential in the Peasants' Revolt (1524-1525) in Germany when thousands tried to obtain civil rights for themselves; for example, the abolition of serfdom, reduction of enforced labor, impartial justice, hunting and fishing rights, owning land. The trouble was that the dukes, barons, civil magistrates were all against these disruptions and the whole country became anarchic and at war. Luther tried to quiet the peasants and told them to go back to their jobs and homes. When his pleas failed, he wrote a tract, *Against the Murderous and Thieving Hordes of Peasants* in which he incited the nobles to "stab, smite, throttle, slay these rabid mad dogs without mercy, with a good conscience to the last ounce of strength, for nothing can be more poisonous, hurtful, or devilish than a rebel. He that shall be slain on the side of law and order is a true martyr before God, earning eternal bliss, he that perishes on the side of rebellion is doomed eternally to hell. Such times are these that a prince shall win heaven by bloodshed sooner than others by prayer." Thus spoke Martin Luther. The nobles did not need to be told twice. There was a frightful carnage and all the peasants were killed. On whose side was God, the Church? Why do we need sides? Luther forgot he too was a rebel.

John Calvin was trained in law in Paris but he also studied religion, the scriptures, the writings of the humanist Erasmus, and the writings of Martin Luther. He began to publish his own tracts and finally had to leave Paris because he was regarded as a heretic by the Catholic ruling class.

He journeyed to Geneva and was invited to stay. They needed someone to help govern and restore religious tranquillity. A religious forest was there growing from the diverse teachings of Luther, Zwingli and others. By this time Calvin was deep into writing and publishing the *Institutes for the Christian Religion*. This monumental book contained a summary of all the chief teachings of Christianity. In a way it was the first Catechism.

Thomas Aquinas (1276), had summarized all of Catholic teaching in his Summa Theological but it was written in Latin, in a scholarly manner for scholars, who were used to argumentation. No one had ever summarized the basic teachings from the New Testament and Church Tradition in a succinct, readable volume for middle-class people. John Calvin, mostly by this work and his years of teaching it in Geneva, was the real architect of the Protestant Reformation.

One of the products of his development of the freedom of salvation and of God's magnificent gift of grace, is Christian predilection and predestination. Grace is freely given by God to whom He so wills. These are the saved.

The great German sociologist Max Weber traces the rise of capitalism in Calvinistic countries to the rise of Protestantism which installed, along with the concept of grace, the idea of the present good life, guaranteed by industry and hard work, the so-called "Protestant Work Ethic."

So skilled was Calvin in indexing and explaining Christian beliefs that he fell heir to the common belief that error has no rights and people who possess the truth for the benefit of all, should impose this truth on all. A Spaniard, Michael Servetus, was an old friend of Calvin's but he had abandoned belief in the Trinity, that there are three distinct persons in God, a belief firmly held by Calvin. Servetus happened to be passing through Geneva and stopped to see Calvin.

He discussed his ideas with Calvin and Calvin advised him to repent and change his heretical thinking. Servetus refused and was quickly tried and burned to death. Calvin also made quick work of extricating Anabaptists from Geneva. They taught that infant baptism was invalid and were followers of Zwingli. Calvin either drove these heretics out of Geneva or executed them.

We have referred earlier to the Church's persecution of so-called witches. This persecution went on well beyond the times of the R eformation and was aided by the teaching of Luther and Calvin. These same teachings accompanied the Puritans to the New World where witches were regularly sought out, tried, and burned. It's amazing what happens to the minds of self-righteous people when they become convinced they possess the truth and are quickly able to discern that the others don't.

"The saved" according to Puritan teaching were the elect who had been overcome with an interior conversion and commitment that was unmistakable, total and life-long. Those who did not get this "awakening" were allowed to be members of the community in New England but could *not* hold office. They were dangerous, untrustworthy, and suspect.

So, women who knew of cures for illnesses from herbs and other concoctions sometimes learned from "savages," and had ways of aiding childbirth that they used in midwifery, became suspect, ultimately accused of heresy, and burned at the stake.

In France, a group of French who followed the teachings of Calvin became known as Huguenots, probably named after Besancon Hugues, an early leader (d. 1532). These French Protestants were universally persecuted through France by the Roman Catholic Church and the French Monarchy. Many were massacred at a wedding that many of them attended on St. Bartholomew's Day (1572). These were civil religious leaders, who were killed.

Many driven out of Rochelle, France, fled to Berlin. This marked the beginning of that city's prominence. They also founded New Rochelle in the New World and were welcome in Holland and England. They were skillful weavers, cloth merchants and artisans of all kinds. Because of their religious beliefs they lost their civil rights and their own nation was diminished because of their loss.

Fortunately for the Jews, a settlement remained in La Chambon, France, where many hundreds of Jews, stayed, passed through, obtained passports during World War II. The Huguenots, mindful of their own persecution for centuries, were loving and warm to "God's chosen people." This story of risk, courage, and daring is told in an awesome portrayal in the movie called *Weapons of the Spirit* by a Jewish survivor.

There are many more stories of the denial and loss of civil rights to almost all religious groups since the reformation. Small groups of people like the Quakers, Amish, and Mennonites have always had a policy of "live and let live"

The Hindus teach "there are many paths," so don't worry about who is right, just walk down the path. Today statistics show that people who attend Church regularly and are more "devout" followers are more prejudiced and unaccepting of others who follow different beliefs or none at all. They seem more biased towards women, minorities, and other races and divergent cultures.

Ministers, priests, and all practitioners of Christianity must ask themselves, with the above paragraph in mind, how untrue and how contradictory this is to the practice of Jesus' admission, "By this shall all men know that you are my disciples, because you love one another."

CHAPTER 9

BIBLICAL INQUIRY
AND HUMAN RIGHTS

A theory is usually a set of interconnected hypotheses or educated guesses that are used to explain and predict in any given area. Good theories not only explain well, in a given time period, but are also fruitful in the development of new and even contradictory theories.

Even a bad theory is better than no theory because people tend to act on theories and observe the results. If the results indicate the theory is not working then the average person, who is sensible, tends to look for a new theory, or at least modifies the one being used.

When new theories appear and seem to contradict old thought patterns and systems, massive reactions usually occur and severe resistance sets in. Frequently vitriolic abuse and attempted restrictions are brought forth to limit or silence the threat. As humans we are intrigued by something new but we also are threatened by different cultures, new science, new schooling, new articles for war, new anything.

Although religion lacks a scientific base and does not feel it is subject to scientific analysis, it often reacts quickly and severely to outside examination and scientific theory that apparently contradict its own messages.

This is obvious in the case of Galileo who said he had scientific proof that the earth revolved around the sun. Up to that point, most everybody thought that the earth was the center of the universe and to say otherwise was to contradict the bible. After all, didn't the sun set and rise on a daily basis? Didn't Josiah hold the sun still until the Israelites were victorious in battle?

The Church was so upset with the publications of Galileo's discoveries that it called him to Rome in 1624 and again in 1632 when he published his *Dialogue on the Great World Systems*. Galileo's blasphemy was referred to the *Inquisition*. He was threatened with torture and ultimately recanted his statements. He was forbidden to publish. Recently Pope John Paul II publicly admitted the Church was wrong and lifted the penalties against Galileo, posthumously. So from the time of is formal trial in 1633 up to 1993, the Church refused to recant when it was obviously wrong. It took only 360 years to rehabilitate Galileo!

Pope Urban VIII, supposedly a man of letters, should have listened to what Augustine had said, 1300 years earlier, "The Bible does not tell you how the heavens go, but how to go to heaven."

Many people aver that the Biblical account of creation in Genesis, Chapter 1 and 2, is an accurate blow by blow description of scientific fact. Obviously it is not, nor does it need to be, to be true. Many stories in the Bible are not historical but the teaching power remains. Even though the stories are not true as happenings in time, the moral of the story remains and this is where **truth** lies. Jesus told the story of the Good Samaritan to illustrate who is my neighbor? He made up the story to get his point across. Does this dilute the message?

To say that the Bible is literal is to obscure in many instances, the true meaning. The Bible, like most timeless literature, uses many literary forms to teach truths. These literary forms range from the poetry of the psalms, the parables of Jesus, the drama of Job, to the history of Kings and to the apocalyptic figurative speech of Ezekiel and

Revelations. To interpret these different styles and forms of literature as literal is not only to do a disservice to Biblical interpretation, but also to befuddle the reader and keep her in a foggy swamp when maybe she should be on a mountain-top with clear vision.

We have more than Galeleo as an example of how the Church obfuscated the research of the Bible. The nineteenth century was awash with new theories in biology from Darwin, economics from Marx, ethics from Nietzsche, to name a few. These invigorating new theories shook the foundations of society, culture, learning and religion.

In 1876, Julius Wellhausen published his *Prolegomena to the History of Israel*. In this logical and cogent presentation Wellhausen outlined his theory that the first six books of the Old Testament (Hexateuch) show four main influences, authors, editors, or traditions. He indicated vocabulary changes, writing styles, descriptions of God, custom variations, points of emphasis, cultic regulations and many others.

Wellhausen posited four major sources, called J.E.D.P. The first was called such because the name of God in some sections is regularly written Yahweh. Another section, with significant other differences, uses the name of Elohim to refer to God. The *D* is abbreviation for Deuteronomist, an editor or school responsible for the book of *Deuteronomy*, but also whose editing appears throughout the other five books of the Hexateuch. Finally, *P* represents the priestly tradition, with its emphasis on genealogies, sacrifices, temple worship, cults, priests, and regulations.

Wellhausen clearly showed that the Pentateuch was not written by a single author, Moses, but by many authors and traditions. His theory better explained many problems associated with "looking for truth" in the Bible. It did not threaten the *truth* but what we formerly held as *truths*.

The German scholarship on the Bible and the history of dogma was picked up in France at the Catholic Institute of Paris. Alfred Loisy began a storm that shook the Vatican. In 1878 he began to apply a vigorous scientific method to ecclesiastical history and Biblical exegesis. He taught that not only should form criticism be used to interpret meaning but dogma should be updated to match with contemporary ways of thinking.

Basically Loisy was applying the concepts of evolutionary theory to the development of dogma. Loisy was never out rightly condemned by Pope Leo XIII, who took a moderate approach to the Bible, and who was a great leader in social thinking and began to publish a series of social encyclical letters. His successor, Pius X, seemed extremely threatened by Loisy in France and George Tyrell in England.

Pius X lumped all their teachings on dogma and biblical interpretation as Modernism and began a systematic condemnation and banning of these teachings. Basically they taught an evolutionary, dynamic view of the universe and said that since nature and the world were not static why should belief systems and dogma also not change to match present conditions and development?

Loisy and Tyrell were branded as heretics and suspended from teaching and were eventually excommunicated from the Church. Their works were placed on the index of forbidden books and they were effectively silenced, lived in humiliation, and condemnation. One of Loisy's most threatened statements was that the Church was an accident that came about because the Second Coming of Christ had not occurred as early Christians thought and predicted. Loisy claimed that the early Christians then thought it necessary to establish an institution, the Church, to keep the teachings alive. This theory shattered the stability-minded Vatican officials and they made short work of Loisy's prominence.

Along with Loisy, a Dominican priest, Marie Joseph La Grange, an outstanding scripture scholar, was silenced and condemned, but he avoided excommunication. He had set up a Biblical School in Jerusalem in 1890. Gradually he began to espouse and teach the historical, critical method of Wellhausen but soon an all out attack from Rome forced him to leave the school he had founded. It is shameful that such a great scholar was ultimately suspected of heresy and forced to live in seclusion.

He is largely responsible for the current catholic revival of interest in Biblical studies and the ecumenical movement which is now somewhat encouraged by Rome. The Catholic Encyclopedia says, "He lifted biblical studies out of mediocrity and by 1943 his school was mentioned with approval in *Divino Afflatre Spiritu*, an encyclical letter of Pius XII." It took the Church only thirty years to get over La Grange, an improvement over the 360 years necessary for Galileo.

The Church had lost the Papal States, the entire center section of Italy, to the reunification movement of Garibaldi in 1870. The Pope referred to himself as "The prisoner of the Vatican" until Mussolini and Pius XI reached a settlement in 1927. This siege mentality applied also to dogma and scripture studies. To question anything was a threat.

The Church should lead in the advance of wisdom and knowledge and should not be threatened by the rise of new theories. After all, Christ said, "The gates of hell shall not prevail against the Church." Why can't the teachings of the Church and the Bible stand examination and close scrutiny? Are the foundation blocks so weak that every questioning must be silenced?

Any theory from a scientific field, needs to be tested to determine if it can stand up to proof. If it fails the test of the laboratory again and again, it proves that the theory needs changing or possibly abandoning.

Yet the Church, by its attitude on Biblical criticism and the evolution of dogma has gone into "a full court press" in the past to silence investigation and testing. Presently the church silences particularly moral theologians who differ with the Vatican. The Roman Church can't allow "liberation theology" and is systematically rooting it out in South America.

People have a right to question, test, and examine all the physical truths of science and they have the same rights in religion. Jesus said, "The truth shall make you free." And if Jesus is "the Way, the Truth, and the Life," can anyone say she has adequately grasped the full meaning? Can't the meaning evolve and can't it be adapted to modern life? Isn't the curtailment of investigation an infringement on human rights? Actually it is a sign of weakness if it cannot change and evolve.

Of course these examples of how the Catholic Church handled Biblical criticism and Modernism is not limited to the Roman Church. Most churches appear to be rigid institutions, which do not tolerate questioners, or what they regard as threats.

Once a religious person thinks she or he possesses the truth, immediately the mind closes to all other ideas, theories, and questions. We have seen how this even results in persecution and death for many who adamantly adapt a different position.

Who can say what great discoveries could have been made out of "biblical meaning" if the full force of scholarship and intelligent study were let free to focus on the Bible from the very beginning? Language. Historical, archaeological, and other focuses can only enhance our knowledge of "meaning" whenever it lies hidden. To seek intuitive explanations and private revelations or frozen meanings when none is necessary is an insult to a revealing God or any intelligent creature of God.

CHAPTER 10
THE USE OF THE "NATURAL LAW" TO CONTINUE BONDAGE

Since the time of Thomas Aquinas (1225 - 1274) the Roman Catholic Church has been a major proponent of the so-called "natural law" theory. There are serious philosophical problems posed by this theory but this type of inconsistency is not the major problem. The major problem affected by this teaching as truth is in the field of morality. To take a shaky or unfounded doctrine as a building block of an ethical system has possible serious ramifications and results.

Aquinas deduces the natural law from the eternal law. In his famous Summa Theologica, Question xci, 1st and 2nd Articles, he says that the whole universe is governed by the eternal law of God. "The very notion of the government of things is God --has the nature of a law and since the divine reason's conception of things is not subject to time., but is eternal ...therefore it is that this kind of law must be called eternal."

Thomas Aquinas goes on to say that humans participate in this eternal law in unique ways. The law is imprinted on them so they "derive their respective inclinations to their proper acts and ends. The human is also provident for itself and others. Therefore it has a share of eternal reason, whereby it has a natural inclination to its proper act and end; and this participation of the eternal law in the rational creature is called the natural law."

It would be unfair to say that Aquinas invented the concept of the natural law. After all there are references to it in the writings of the great Roman Orator Cicero and in the frequently quoted reference of St. Paul in Romans where he condemns homosexuality as a perversion of nature. The text of Romans 1:20f; His invisible attributes -- have been visible -- to the eye of reason. But, because some have not paid attention to this obvious law "God has given them up to shameful passions. Their women have exchanged natural intercourse for unnatural, and their men in turn, giving up natural relations with women, burn with lust for one another; males behave indecently with males, and are paid in their own persons the fitting wage of such perversions."

Paul states unequivocally that homosexuality is a perversion and intrinsically wrong. This same sort of statement is made by the Catholic Church about using what is called "unnatural birth control." This type of birth control uses devices, like condoms and diaphragms, to impede fertilization or pills to alter the reproductive process. Any interference with the natural process must be regarded as immoral and sinful.

Part of this proof stems from Aristotle who made great use of the teleological argument. Each thing in creation has a specific end or objective and to reach its proper goal and function is important to the proper action of the universe. All link together in harmony, reaching their own ends, working for the good of the whole!

We examine the foundations of this doctrine of the natural law by stating that there is no such thing to start with. If there is any law in nature, humans have been interfering with it since they reached consciousness and awareness.

Since humans discovered fire they have been trying to keep warm from it even thought nature says it is cold, cold enough to freeze. Although we are born, naturally, without clothes our parents and g uardians quickly cover us to protect us from the elements and danger or for cultural reasons.

Periodically people try to get back to nature in some form or other but they do this only temporarily and frequently take along a great many "inventions" to aid them. They need food, clothing, matches, flashlights, compasses, knives, axes, water, blankets, and maybe guns.

To say that there is natural law seems to go against common sense. There seems to be repetitive happenings in nature that give predictability and constitute laws. Actually these "laws" are made by humans, stemming from observation, analysis and synthesis. These laws, which we use to explain and predict behavior, are subject to constant revision, updating, and in sometimes, total abandonment.

The paradigms, theorems and laws of one era are succeeded by new updated "laws.". Laws are words, formulas, descriptions of observable reality. They state what we observe at a given time with knowledge we have.

The finer instruments we develop to look at the heavens or microscopic life lead us to see and believe more than we ever dreamed was "really there." The better tools lead to more discoveries, more wonders, more and better questions. Then we revise our conceptual framework with which we describe reality and rewrite our "laws."

It is true that there is a certain order and harmony to the universe but does that mean there is a law? Frequently this order and harmony is totally disrupted by an earthquake, a flood, a tornado, or a hurricane. Then what happened to the law? There was no law there so it didn't go away.

Let us examine the concept that the reproductive sexual organs have been made for a certain purpose and if we interfere with this we are doing evil. This is not necessarily true. The sexual organs have diverse purposes, only one of them reproductive. The sexual organs are a seat of immense pleasure and also an instrument for showing affection and love. To say that they have *only* the function of reproduction seems to contradict "nature."

Declaring that it wrong to interfere with the normal flow of semen trying to reach the ovum would make it wrong to fly, dam rivers, send water to homes, take care of waste, take medicine, wear glasses, wear clothes, drive cars, build houses, watch TV. We spend most of our lives overcoming "nature." The first inventions like the wheel, knives, and clubs were ways of overcoming and conquering "nature." Is a condom that much different from a dam?

There is the argument that it is wrong to use something for a purpose different that for what it was intended. This argument is patently full of holes. We could say our noses were made for breathing and smelling but can't they be used to hold our glasses, along with our ears, made for hearing.

There is recent evidence that homosexuality is possibly genetic. There is a different drive in gays and lesbians and if this is true are they not acting naturally if they prefer a sexual partner of the same sex? The fact that this sort of drive affects only a minority does not matter. Not all are "born" baseball players, skaters, musicians, cooks, geniuses. If we are a minority, frequently the world applauds our diversity. It may be an accomplished opera singer, violin player, dancer, physician, airplane designer. What then if my sexual proclivities are different?

To get back to *birth* control. A number of years ago Pope John XXIII commissioned a study on the possibility of changing the teaching of the church on this subject. After several years of intense study a majority of the commission, including theologians, doctors, lay-people, scripture scholars, concluded that the possibility of change was present and necessary. A minority dissented and Pope Paul VI was afraid to withstand this vocal minority. He committed a wrong here that infected permanent damage on the Church.

The Church taught that usury, lending money for interest, was wrong. The Church changed this teaching and itself operates banks that practice usury. The fact that the Church always taught something doesn't make the Church right. Witness the Church's teaching on Galileo that changed.

On birth control, the Church's present attitude is immovable and tragic. The world is overpopulated, economically unable to support an expanding population. Many parents are in dire straights, unable to cope with a large family and the Church makes them feel guilty for practicing birth control.

The Church, with its inhuman attitude towards gays and lesbians has brought many persons to the brink of despair, laden with guilt, trying to overcome urges that are "natural." The Church's teaching on birth control and homosexuality is cruel and in direct opposition to its mission.

It is time for the Church to say it is wrong, has been wrong and to right the wrongs. It is time to say good-bye to the "natural law" theory and develop a "humane law" good for the growth and development of humans.

CHAPTER 11

SLAVERY AND THE CHURCH

Slavery probably started when humans began to live as agrarians and city dwellers. Then it became profitable to have others producing for you, either food, clothing, mechanical instruments or taking care of family needs. Slavery existed in all early societies and most societies took slavery for granted and had laws and rules governing this practice.

When Jesus lived, the Romans made slaves of the Jews and the Jews had practiced slavery, off and on, since their beginnings as outlined in Genesis. Jesus never said a word about the institution of slavery but it would seem from his attitude toward the downtrodden and the persecuted that his words could be interpreted that he was against slavery.

However, no early writer or preacher seems to have accepted that meaning. It seems incongruous that a God who supposedly created all men equal would not be against slavery and make His wishes known. But He didn't.

In the Old Testament God makes rules of all kinds, even dietary regulations, how to handle different types of uncleanness and many practices relating to proper worship. There are some regulations about how slaves are to be treated and dealt with and in some instances, freed. Yet, the institution itself is not condemned.

St. Paul, the first great theologian of the Church took slavery as a given and although he railed against many practices and moralities it never entered his mind that slavery is an evil.

Is there anyone today who would try to justify the practice of slavery? The total *owning* of another human who has no rights seems to be a sin against humanity. Yet, the Church, and its heavy emphasis on the "natural law," did not see slavery as against the "natural law." St. Paul sees homosexuality as unnatural and slavery as natural.

St. Paul talks of the slavery of sin but not the slavery of the body. He seems to think the latter is righteous as in Galatians 4:28 he compares the new law, to a child born of a free woman, and the old law, to a child born of a slave. Hagar is Abraham's slave woman and bears him a child, Ishmael. When Isaac is born of Sarah, Sarah is jealous of Hagar and Ishmael and orders Abraham to drive her and the child out in the desert. Abraham regrets this action but complies. Hagar is only a slave woman and her child should not be around even to contest inheritance from Abraham.

As Paul states in Gal 4:30 "Yet what does scripture say? 'Drive out the slave and her son, for the son of the slave shall not share the inheritance with the son of the free woman.'" This despicable act of unseemly treatment is regarded by Paul as admirable and worthy of a great lesson For him it teaches the munificence of God's saving grace. But what does it say about slavery? It seems to indicate that slaves deserve bad treatment and if one as worthy as Abraham is allowed to deal so with them, what lesson does this teach?

In several other passages Paul specifically mentions slaves being obedient. In Colossian's 3:22 he states, "Slaves, give entire obedience to your earthly masters, not merely to catch their eye or curry favor with them, but with single-mindedness, out of reverence for the Lord." And in 4:1, "Masters, be just and fair to your slaves, knowing that you too have a master in heaven."

In 1Corinthians 7:20, Paul seems to argue for the permanence of slavery on the basis that it is better not to disturb the status quo.

The Church: A History of Injustice 67

"Everyone should remain in the condition in which he was called. Were you a slave when you were called? Do not let that trouble you?" In this, as in other passages, Paul seems to regard service to Christ, as being a form of slavery and since this is a good thing for Paul what's the big problem with earthly servitude? Very few Christians today could defend such an attitude especially if it concerns the plight of others.

The shortest letter attributed to Paul is to Philemon. The subject matter is Onesimus, a run-a-way slave whom Paul has converted and baptized and is now sending back to Philemon. He begs Philemon not to punish the slave but to treat him nicely. Paul tells Philemon he will make it all up to him later. Paul basically canonizes the institution of slavery, provided we are good masters.

This same argument was used by slave-holders in the South at the time of Civil War in the United States. They stated that the slaves were better off under their Christian care and freeing them would be an act of disservice. Having made little attempt to educate or train them, they made use of a self-fulfilling prophecy in making it exceedingly difficult to succeed.

So early Christians maintained a double standard, baptizing slaves and making them "spiritual" equals but keeping them in bodily bondage. It became necessary for Christian theologians to justify this bondage. The classic argument was brought forth by St. Augustine, the fifth Century Bishop of Hippo in Africa. He adopted the major lines of his predecessors: 1)people before the Fall were equal; (2)the universal sinfulness entailed by the Fall required institutions of coercion, including slavery; (3)slaves should be obedient and masters kindly; and (4)sin itself is the worst slavery, no matter what one's civil status might be.

Augustine went so far as correlate servitude with present sin, maybe bad karma. "Perpetual servitude does not deface a man, save by the decree of God, who is never unjust, and who knows how to impose appropriate punishments on different sinners."

With key thinkers like Augustine leading the way the institution of slavery lasted until almost the twentieth century.

Christians monarchs like Ferdinand and Isabella, who sponsored Columbus, also fostered slavery in the new world. The Spanish throne was so bent on converting the "savages" of the new world that they saw a refusal to convert to Catholicism as signing their own death warrant. They wiped out whole tribes and nations. Then they brought slaves to replace them.[10]

By the time England gained ascendancy in the new world a religious division had split Christendom. Many Christians who were persecuted in their own land came to America to practice their faith in freedom. Many of these Christians: Anglicans, Methodists, Baptists, had no problem dealing with slavery. They bought and sold slaves and saw no contradiction.

We all like to rationalize our behavior and to justify it to ourselves and others. Even if it is reprehensible we seek a way to explain it away. We blame our weakness, our parents, our peers, our culture, or the evil spirit. "The devil made me do it."

The early Christians who settled this country were torn between evangelizing the Negro slaves and ignoring the possibilities of conversion. If they were to be converted then weren't they human and deserved freedom? If they needed to study the catechism and the Bible shouldn't they be taught to read? If they were taught to read wouldn't they read other literature that might forment unrest and the desire for freedom?

They solved this problem by teaching slaves who converted that their true reward awaited them in heaven. Since they were "all one in Christ" there was no need for them to get upset about being slaves and many slave owners reported that converted slaves became more docile following St. Paul's teachings: "Be subject to your master as to the Lord."

The Church, the Catholic and Protestant Church, along with Muslim nations have all condoned, fostered and perpetuated slavery. St. Paul says in Romans that those who disobey the "natural law" are without excuse. Yet he did not see the incongruities of slavery and humanness.

Certainly the full development of humanness cannot take place under conditions of slavery. In slavery the human is *owned* by another human. To perpetuate this myth as being righteous, slaves had to be viewed as less than human, thus justifying the procedure.

---

[10] First the Pilgrims fell upon their knees, then they fell upon the aborigines.

If slaves were kept ignorant, forced to work long hours, fed poor food, given sub-standard living conditions, mistreated sexually, driven like animals, how many could rise into a feeling of human worth and dignity? Did they not then themselves justify being called "heathens", "pagans", and savages".

The Church has never admitted its role in the perpetuation of this degradation and the results are still with us, evidenced by our slums and widespread poverty. The white Church seems barely interested in converting these blacks to Christianity, especially if they have their "own churches." But the social conditions that have evolved from slavery have not been treated adequately and the question is what has been done throughout the centuries - what will the Church do? And when?

CHAPTER 12

THE AMERICAN INDIANS AND

CHRISTIANITY

We come now in our study of the Church and Civil and Human Rights to the Church's part in the total annihilation of Indian Civil Rights and the almost total annihilation of a whole people. When the Christian settlers came to the land, now called the United States, there were indeed many nations of Indians indigenous to the territory. They had lived here for thousands of years. They soon found that the struggles they had before the arrival of the Christian white man were nothing compared with the death struggle that ensued.

Some of the Iroquois tribes had been living in the northern U.S. for at least 5,000 years. The Hopi Indians had been living in the junction of Colorado, New Mexico, Arizona, and Utah for at least 10,000 years. Some archeologists estimate the Hopi arrival at 40,000 years ago. Many Indians do not claim to have arrived at all. They just are or were.

When I was in grade school I was taught that Columbus "discovered America" October 12, 1492. And what a great event it was touted as. Here were the savage Indians, living in the woods, not building houses, not clearing the land, and not having a national government. They hunted for a living using animals they killed to eat and to make garments from. They didn't have guns and they didn't drink alcohol. Worst of all they were savages in need of civilization and conversion.

The Indians mostly welcomed the settlers and tried to teach them how to survive in the wilderness. They didn't think they had been discovered nor the land they lived on. How does one claim to "discover" an inhabited land? And how does one quickly define the "found" group as primitive and savage?

The Europeans used Noah Webster's type of definitions, which evolved out of their adaptations of meaning. Webster in his 1828 edition of An American Dictionary of the English Language says:

> Civilization: n. The act of civilizing, or the state of being civilized: the state of being refines in manners, from the grossness of savage life, and improved in acts of learning.

> Savage: n. A human being in his native state if rudeness, one who is untaught, uncivilized or without cultivation of mind or manners.

The savages of America, when uncorrupted by the vices of civilized men are remarkable for their hospitality for strangers, and for their truths, fidelity and gratitude to their friends, but implacably cruel and revengeful to their enemies.

> Savagism: n. The state of rude uncivilized men; the state of men in their native wilderness and rudeness.

Actually, from reading the definition of savage we see that Indians were, in some ways, the same or better then white settlers. They didn't need or want to be taught how to "act civilized."

The white people from Europe, who were all Christians of one sort or another, could never convince the Indiana to imitate them except for teaching them to switch to guns and to drink alcohol. The white Christians, many who were fired up with new brands of Christianity, came to America to avoid persecution and to practice their own type of devotion, uninhibited. Yet, many of these same people were hell-bent to convert all that did not follow their practices. They thought the savage Indians, once they heard the message of salvation, that the Lord Jesus Christ had come to redeem them, would repent of their sins, start clearing the forests, get baptized and come to Church.

The Indians already "had religion." They believed the earth was sacred and hence not "theirs". They thought plants, animals, streams and rocks were sacred. They respected nature, mother earth and even the animals they killed to eat and to make garments. They prayed, sang religious songs and helped one another. They didn't need converting, being saved or being civilized.

The white man was astounded at how backward the Indians were. They were basically a society that hunted, had few laws and rules and seemed to function without lawyers. They had "chiefs" but these chiefs were different for different situations, such as a chief for hunting, one for war, another for peace or territory. Being a chief did not mean you were an autocratic ruler but a true leader and model, a person to respect. Many were women, something unheard of among the whites.

The white man who slowly began to inhabit the Indian's land thought the Indians would be very impressed with the way Europeans did things. They has advanced way beyond the Indian Culture. In their minds not only was this a fact, but also part of the Divine Plan. Whatever happened in history, in war and peace, in invention, in philosophy, or science, resulted from a Divine Plan.

After all they were following the orders of Yahweh in Genesis. "And God said, 'Let us make man in our image, after our likeness, and let them have dominion over the fish of the sea, and over the fowl of the air, and over the cattle and over all the earth, and over every creeping thing that creepeth upon the earth.'" Genesis 1:26

"And God blessed them and said unto them, 'Be fruitful and multiply, and replenish the earth, and subdue it: and have dominion over the fish, fowl, and every living thing.'" Gen. 1:28

The message found in the beginnings of Judaism and ultimately its branch Christianity delivered a clear message that man was in charge of the earth and needed to "subdue it." This command had a tremendous influence on western civilization, which became the seat of technology, invention and ultimately the western world powers. When the white European came he brought massive change, inventions, rules, rulers, fire-power, many unheard of diseases and Christianity. When you were subjected, bought or discovered you were expected to be smart enough to buy the package. It was like running into the "godfather" among the Mafia when he made you "an offer you couldn't refuse."

The Catholic rulers of Spain, Ferdinand and Isabella, who graciously sponsored Columbus' trips to America, also sent missionaries to convert the heathen Indians to Catholicism. They later offered the Jews and Moors who lived in the Spain three options: (1) convert to Catholicism; (2) leave; or (3) die. The soldiers who came to the Americas from Spain had the same mission and principles. When people are certain of their beliefs they frequently pose dangers for other who are unsuspecting of their maniacal zeal.

The Spanish missionaries who accompanied the Spanish soldiers often tried to caution this zeal but were mostly unsuccessful. The Spanish saw that these savage Indians were not the least interested in becoming slaves to a progress they did not want. It would be the "Will of God" that they should die.

This same rationale eventually persuaded all the Christian Colonies, almost to a man, to drive the Indian further and further westward. They made treaties and then broke them. After all they were only savages. They could see that the Indians rejected the idea of clearing the forest, becoming gentlemen farmers, and gathering in cities. This plan was the manifest will of the Divine and therefore anyone rejecting this plan deserved bad treatment, torture and yes, death.

As Jesus said, "and thus is wisdom justified by all her children." Here we see the Christian Church which formed the leaders and the people of Christendom, teaching an arrogance that no one can abide, and in the name of Christ, the peacemaker, bringing death and destruction to all who do not convert. The Christians, who were once persecuted, invaded the land of Israel to take the holy places back from the "infidel" and killed everyone in Jerusalem and thousands of Jews and Moslems on the way.

Thousand were slaughtered by the Inquisition, by the Reformation and when then "Christians" came to the America they did it again and in the name of progress, in the name of the King and in the name of Jesus.

These grave injustices have never been fully examined, even acknowledged. They have been glossed over in the history books. The worst crime was committed in Hollywood through the movies. The Indian was always depicted as the bad guy, cunning, untrustworthy, unintelligent, nothing more than a savage who deserved to die. And die he did, slaughtered in film, killed by the good guys, the infantry, the messengers of the United States government, the messenger of Divine Providence.

It is time we repent of what we have done to these innocent people. We have broken every commandment of common sense against them. We have stolen, lied, enslaved, pillaged, robbed, and killed.

We need to get off our high horse and see what indignities we have committed against a helpless people. Let us seek the truth, acknowledge it and act on it.

It may be that we are the ones who are wrong and we need to take another look at what the Indians tried to teach us and are still crying out. This cry is manifest in this excerpt from A Basic Call to Consciousness (Iroquois) Address to the Western World delivered at the 1977 UN Conference on Indigenous Peoples.

> In the beginning we were told that the human beings who walk about on the Earth have been provided with all the things necessary for life. We were instructed to carry a love for one another, and to show great respect for all the beings of this Earth. We were shown that our life exists with the tree life, that our well being depends on the well being of the Vegetable Life, that we are close relatives of the four-legged beings.
>
> The Original instructions direct that we who walk about on Earth are to express a great respect, an affection and a gratitude toward all the spirits which create and support Life . . . .When people cease to respect and express gratitude for these many things, then all life will be destroyed, and human life on this planer will come to an end.
>
> To this day the territories we still hold are filled with trees, animals, and the other gifts from the Creation. In these places we still receive our nourishment from our Mother Earth . . . .
>
> The Indo-European people who have colonized our lands have shown very little respect for the things that create and support Life. We believe that these people ceased their respect for the world a long time ago. Many thousands of years ago all the people of the world believed in the same Way of Life, that of harmony with the Universe. All lived according to the Natural Ways.
>
> Today the [human] species of Man is facing a question of [its] very survival . . . . The way of life know as Western Civilization is on a death path on which their own culture has no viable answers. When f

aced with the reality of their own destructiveness, they can only go forward into areas of more efficient destruction.

The air is foul, the waters poisoned, the tree dying, the animals are disappearing, We think even the systems of weather are changing. Our ancient teaching warned us that if Man interfered with the Natural laws, these things would come to be. When the last of the Natural Way of Life is gone, all hope for human survival will be gone with it. And our Way of Life is fast disappearing, a victim of the destructive processes.

The technologies and social systems which destroyed the animal and the plant life are destroying the Native people . . . . We know there are many people in the world who can quickly grasp the intent of our message. But our experience has taught us that there are few who are willing to seek out a method for moving toward any real change.

The majority of the world does not fine its roots in Western culture or tradition. The majority of the world finds its root in the Natural World, and it is the Natural World, and the traditions of the Natural World, which must prevail.

We must all consciously and continuously challenge every model, every program, and every process that the West tried to force upon us. . . . The people who are living on this planet need to break with the narrow concept of human liberation, and begin to see liberation as something that needs to be extended to the whole of the Natural World. What is needed is the liberation of all things that support sacred web of Life.

The Native people of the Western Hemisphere can contribute to the survival potential of the human species. The majority of our peoples still live in accordance with the traditions, which find their roots in the Mother Earth. But the Native people have need of a forum in which our voice can be heard. And we need alliances with the other people of the world to assist in our struggle to regain and maintain our ancestral lands and to protect the Way of Life we follow.

The traditional Native people hold the key to the reversal of the processes in Western Civilization, which hold the promise of unimaginable future suffering and destruction. Spiritualism is the highest form of political consciousness. And we, the Native people of the Western Hemisphere, are among the world's surviving proprietors of that kind of consciousness . . . . Our culture is among the most ancient continuously existing cultures in the world. We are the spiritual guardians of this place. We are here to impart the message.

The word civilization has its roots in the Latin word civis which mean citizen. The Romans had conquered the whole known world and made Roman citizenship an option for qualified conquered people. St. Paul, a Jew was proud he was a Roman citizen and appealed to the court of Caesar for a fair trial. All non-citizens were classified as barbarians. It didn't matter whether you were educated, skilled, had manners, or even money. If you were not Roman you were a barbarian.

Humans are victims of tunnel vision, of being blind-sided, what is technically called Ethnocentrism. This leads a given culture, nation, tribe into thinking its culture, ethos, knowledge is better than any other. It can lead to an overwhelming desire to convert others to it, force it on them, and eradicate them if they do not accept. It also leads to fear which prompts exclusion segregation, discrimination, bigotry, and the violence necessary to maintain the sense of superiority.

Christians must realize they, all together as Catholics, Protestants and Orthodox represent only a third of the world's population. They are a minority and are not necessarily "right." The Hindus teach that there are many paths. The Koran advises Muslims to be tolerant of Jews and Christians, an admonition not always adhered to.

When Jesus spoke the Beatitudes, it is noted that two of them refer to Justice. The King James translation, reads: "Blessed are they who hunger and thirst for Justice." (Mt 5:6) and "Blessed are they who suffer persecution for the justice sake." (Mt 5:10)

The Christians who invaded the Americas certainly did not practice justice toward the Indians, We still can't figure out why they don't just get civilized Since they aren't Romans they are barbarians. We have defined them out of our consciousness.

The key virtue of Christian life is supposed to be charity. "By this shall all men know that you are my disciples, because you love one another." (Jn 13:35) Can we claim we know not what we do?

CHAPTER 13

PRESENT ATTITUDE OF THE CHURCH

AND WOMEN'S RIGHTS

On May 30, 1994, Pope John Paul II came as close as possible to defining "excathedrs" (a solemn definition of faith from the chair of Peter, infallible and irretractable) that women cannot be ordained priests in the Roman Catholic Church.

His exact words were:

> Wherefore, in order that all doubt may be removed regarding a matter of great importance, a matter which pertains to the Church's divine constitution itself, in virtue of my ministry of confirming the brethren I declare that the Church has no authority whatsoever to confer priestly ordination on women and that this judgment is to be definitively held by all the Church's faithful.

The Pope is echoing a long tradition in Church circles that effectively teaches the inferiority of women, that they cannot possibly represent Christ as a priest. Many of the American Catholic bishops have tried somehow to weaken this blatant sexist teaching by saying " women are still called to leadership position," and some other forms of ministry, usually unstated and unspecified.

Although women cannot become priests but are still called upon to exercise leadership in the Church, is basically ridiculous, and in the face of it, an outright lie. Power lies with the pope and then with the bishops and Cardinals. To say in one breath that women are not allowed in this group and men say " but they are still called to leadership position," is clearly contradictory.

The American Catholic bishops tried for eight years to publish a controversial pastor letter on women entitled "one in Christ Jesus." They tried every which we to make women feel better about their role in the Church, and still insist they cannot be priests. In other words you are A, equal, and b not equal. The most uneducated logician knows that the principal of contradiction is involved here and the statement cannot stand. It took the bishops eight years to come to this conclusion.

Of course, millions of women have been thought submission, to take a secondary place voluntarily and to yield to the power of patriarchy. For it is truly patriarchy that rules all the seats of power: political, financial, educational, medical and ecclesiastical. For centuries women have been uneducated, secluded, captives and slaves. They will continue to be sold until they revolt. As Frederick Douglas said, " the limits of tyrants are proscribed by the endurance of those whom they suppress."

Until women rise up and refuse to support with words, submission and money, an institution that clearly demeans them, they will continue to be oppressed. This is what happen in the United States to black people and what happened in South Africa.

The trouble is that this oppression has gone on so long and is now so much part of the culture and system that many women do not even know it. Men take advantage of it and often don't know it. If you point this out to these people they become uneasy, belligerent, and defensive. They refuse to listen and often-expressed countering data with statements like: " It's part of the divine plan, it's God's will. You are going against nature. "

The real question is: are women human? If men and women are old human they should be able to develop their full potential, according to their own abilities, desires and inner maturation. Law or custom should not determine who can be a doctor, firemen, president, pope, or butcher. Yet the Church, which presents itself as a leader in ethics and societal norms, continues to oppress women and refer to them as some sort of creatures with a peculiar nature that is better than animal but less than man.

The Catholic encyclopedia, 1986 edition say:

> "In the assembly of the Church, by tradition and teaching, women are to be silent, for the burden of proclaiming the word is the function of men."

the same publication goes on to say:

> in the modern Church it has been consistent teaching that, while the part women are to take in the service of God is expanded to ministries, they are called to be " disciples and collaborators," but not ordained ministers, as Pope Paul VI has declared. They are called to seek greater leadership roles, expanded education and collaborative work in the apostolate of all.

The most recent pronouncements have not improve on this double-talk which supposedly is so will-written and subtle that even intelligent women cannot quite grasp the message -you are inferior and must accept that.

One of the recent changes that has terrified pope John Paul II was the November 11, 1992, decision of the general synod of the Church of England to approve the ordination of women to the priesthood. This that happened earlier in the United States but now has come to pass in England, much to the dismay of conservative Anglicans and the Pope.

Recently the Vatican has been trying to push ecumenism with the Church of England, trying to reunite with a group most like them in doctrine and ritual. Now the Pope cannot even consider reunion, except through the defection of conservatives who seek union with unchangeable Rome. What a strange phenomenon-many Roman Catholic priests are becoming Anglicans so they can give up celibacy, and many Anglicans are finding their Church too lax and are heading for Rome. And all because of women! The Catholic priests want to marry them but not to ordain them and the strict Anglicans cannot relish the thought of such an in dignity as to be the two serve God alongside of women.

Recently Rome granted permission for the American Catholic Church to print and distribute the new catechism. The only problem is that the Vatican in the like inconclusive language which was supposed to indicate that scripture and Church doctrine are meant not only for men but also for " women". the Vatican says that the generic use of " men " includes women. Well, we know that wasn't true in the united states, since women couldn't even vote until an amendment was has in 1920. Nor does " men" include women when it come to ordination.

The Catholic Church seems to be terrified of even using the personal pronoun she. Is Christ's promise that " the gates of hell will not prevail against the Church, " in grave jeopardy if the Church indicates that female are equal to males?

It is odd that in many instances the present Church has failed to see that many things in Scripture are culture bound and changeable. Jesus changed some of the rules of the old testament and the Church changed the day of worship from Saturday to Sunday. They changed their minds on usury and Galileo. The changed their minds on slavery. Paul recommended that slaves obey their masters. Would he do so today?

Bishop Shelby Spong and Anglican Bishop from Newark, wrote in 1991:

> In Separate ways, but with a patriarchal consistency, the various Christian leaders accepted a definition of women the preclude the possibility that a woman could represent God at the altar. Without daring to say so outright, they were nevertheless suggesting that women are not created in the image of God.

Many Church goers like to dismiss the petitions and demands of feminists women who seek equality of opportunity. They refer to these women as: radicals, secularist, materialists, communists, and anarchists. They think they can silence them by falling them names and labeling them. Along side the name-callers are the radical right Christians who espouse one form or another of fundamentalism. These groups basically teach that the bible is to be interpreted literally, despite the fact that frequently Jesus himself said, "let me tell you a story."

For years the Catholic Church considered Christian fundamentalists a bit off the mark. Now they are uniting with them over abortion rights, the emancipation of women, prayer in school and other issues. Maybe the ecumenical movement will be aided by this strange alliance.

Yet women need to see through all these claims of certitude and dogma. As Rosemary Ruter [11] says:

> The critical principle of feminist theology is the affirmation and promotion of the full humanity of women. Whatever denies, diminishes or distorts the full humanity of women's, therefore, to be appraised as not redemptive.

It would seem that for the cards to the laid clearly on the table, the issues stated openly and declarations made as to whose side you are on. Double agents, equivocators, deceivers are not needed.

This world is full of real problems that must be solved and yet we waste untold energy keeping women, minorities, and homosexuals in certain restricted areas and unlimited opportunities. Why? What is the payoff? How long can we do this with impunity?

I would like to point out an area in which the Christians, Moslems and Jews of the world could have a tremendous influence. They should declare themselves against the mutilation of women, particularly genital mutilation, a widespread practice especially in Africa. The Roman Catholic Church, which decries war, infanticide, and abortion has said nothing publicly about this crippling cruelty to girls and women.

Genital mutilation, the cutting of the clitoris and other female genitalia, was begun supposedly to protect females from men other than their husbands. It destroys sexual pleasure and desire, imperils childbirth, destroys the body and destroys the spirit.

Millions of females suffer indescribable pain, disease and death because of this cruel practice and must stop. The Churches could, with a unified, concerted effort bring this about. Such extreme cruelty should no longer be allowed. It is clearly immoral and wrong and any institution that preaches morality should include eradicating this practice.

It is time for the Christian Church to reexamine Paul's teaching to the Galatians in reference to race, religion and sexuality.

---

[11] A noted Catholic theologian and feminist author who teaches at a seminary in Chicago.

"It is through faith that you are all sons of God in union with Christ Jesus. Baptized into union with him you have all put on Christ like a garment. There is no such thing as Jew and Greek, slave and freeman, male and female; for you are all one person in Christ Jesus. So if you belong to Christ, you are the "issue" of Abraham and heirs by virtue of the promise." (Gal 3:26-29)

Perhaps the Roman Catholic Church is asking the wrong questions. This can be true in science, industry, politics, and academics. Instead of asking can women be equal, ordained and elected, the Church should be asking what are the qualifications necessary to show equality, be ordained or get elected. If gender has proven to be an ineffective and unfair way to rule the secular or business world, why is it fair in the Church? How many excellent teachers, preacher, and ministers of the gospel have we lost because of this exclusiveness? Isn't it time to get on to solving real problems?

CHAPTER 14

HOMOSEXUALITY AND

THE CHURCH TODAY

Frequently, bad philosophy and theology have stemmed from bad or incorrect biology, astrology, medicine, and pathology. Aristotle, Augustine, Thomas Aquinas to name only a few have reached erroneous opinions about the essence, the ontology of women, based on erroneous assumptions about sex. Aristotle thought women had nothing to do with the conception of children. They merely carried and nurtured them after the male deposited the child during intercourse. Aquinas said women were conceived during a moist sough wind. Augustine thought the story of Adam and Eve were literal and from this he developed his misogynist attitude toward women.

It is no wonder than, that we find an erroneous position by the Roman Catholic Church, The Fundamentalists, and large numbers of mainstream Protestants, on the question of homosexuality. For years the medical and psychiatric professions supported the Church position. Homosexuality, the sexual attraction and preference for a member of the same sex has been looked upon as: a matter of voluntary choice, a pathological condition brought about by poor parenting and modeling, a sin against nature and God's commands.

There is sufficient evidence now to show that sexual preference stems from genetic material and one cannot get rid of it by will power, divine help, medicine, therapy, or aging. The imprint is in the brain, from early on in gestation and could be classified as 'natural', for those bearing it.

Because of this research and further evidence the American Psychiatric Association in 1973 removed homosexuality from the Diagnostic and *Statistical Manual of Mental Disorders.* In the *Atlantic Monthly,* March 1993, Chandler Burr stated:

> Five decades of psychiatric evidence demonstrates that homosexuality is immutable and nonpathological, and a growing body of more recent evidence implicates biology in the development of sexual orientation.

Despite these discoveries by scientists and medical practitioners the Church continues to admonish homosexuals to straighten up and become moral. This type of moral teaching has fostered widespread bias and practice against these people. The true evil and sin resides in those who harbor prejudice and demonstrate bigotry.

Father John J. McNeill, S. J., long an advocate of these persecuted individuals says in his book, *The Church and the Homosexual* (1976):

> As in many other areas of moral philosophy, the advances made in philosophical anthropology, where the human is understood along dynamic lines of self-creative freedom rather than static essence, serve as a basis for a cultural reexamination of the traditional condemnation of homosexuality derived from the natural law approach of the Scholastics.

To reiterate, it took centuries for the Church finally to admit Galileo was right. To say that usury was no longer forbidden, and that Biblical criticism could move ahead. It is time now for the Church to examine its formal teaching on morality regarding homosexuality. It is time to change its attitude and practice about women.

The fact that something has been taught for many centuries does not justify continuing, once it's been proven erroneous. Jesus himself changed many of the rules and regulation of Moses and condemned the Scribes and Pharisees for their strict interpretation of the law.

There are very few scriptural references to homosexuality but these texts are used to justify a practice that is clearly wrong now. The Church has fostered and created an atmosphere in which hatred and the mistreatment of homosexuals have resulted in ridicule, beatings and murder, all in the name of justifiable homicide and the administering of divine wrath.

The Hindus say that if there appears to be a contradiction in the Scriptures you obviously have not yet found the true meaning. I think this applies to the few oblique or clear references to homosexuality in the Bible.

One of the references most frequently used is from Genesis XIX. Even the name sodomy comes from this story because it involves the description of the destruction of Sodom and Gomorrah for their sins. It is not clear why the story indicates God was displeased with their conduct. The tow angels sent to warn Lot and his family were truly in danger, but is this why the cities were destroyed? Why did Lot, a good man, offer his daughters for abuse? Was this acceptable? Were the daughters morally right in getting their father drunk and raping him incestuously? Are these the good people God was trying to save?

Certainly there must be something else in the story that requires our attention other than the condemnation of homosexuality, which actually never takes place. These early stories of Genesis were told to teach truths, even if the stories themselves are not true. Sin will be punished, good triumphs over evil, God rules the world, get on the side of righteousness; these and other truths or myths are contained in the story. To single out homosexuality as condemned in these passages is farfetched.

Leviticus XX:13 does indeed point out "if a man has intercourse with a man as with a woman, both commit an abomination. They must be put to death." Leviticus also says many other things to which no one in the Christian religion pays any attention.

In the same chapter, we read that if a man has sex with a menstruating woman, they both are to be cut off from the people. A person who called up ghosts and spirits is to be put to death. Probably this is the source of the Salem witch burnings. In the same section it says "when anyone reviles his father and his mother, he must be put to death." Lev20:9 Obviously we no longer follow this, so why get excited about rules on homosexuality? They are to be examined, along with other practices, in the light of new evidence and cultural changes, not to mention common sense.

A key scriptural reference to homosexuality in the New Testament is found in Romans 1:24. If you begin reading at verse 18 you see that Paul is telling the Romans that the attributes of God are clearly seen in nature and that those who ignore these clear messages and symbols will be given up by God to their own vile desires. In this passage homosexuality as such is not condemned but only those heterosexuals who have turned away from the truth and have resorted to homosexual "acts". This seems to be what is condemned, and in this case it is a punishment by God. Perhaps it is the Hindu ides of bad Karma bringing bad results.

The tern sexual pervert is used in 1 Cor 6:9 and 1 Tim 1:10 in some translation and others say those who sin against nature but it is not clear if homosexuality is meant, and then again is it a homosexual act by a heterosexual or a homosexual life-style that is condemned?

To use these few obscure references from the Bible to condemn and ostracize a large group of people who may be genetically so disposed is erroneous and sinful.

Ontology, the study of being, the essences of things, has had a tremendous influence on the destiny of women. If women "are" a certain way by birth then they can be treated a certain way. If some segments of the population are born a certain way in sexual orientation what are we to say about their treatment? In one case we have used philosophy wrongfully to relegate women to the position of slaves and then denied even the possibility of ontology acting in homosexuality.

Since we have upgraded our genetics, biology, and psychiatry in regard to homosexuality, it is time to upgrade scriptural interpretation and application, to upgrade the assumption of morality and of our daily practice in human relations.

The Brooklyn Tablet, a Catholic paper said in January, 1976 that we need "a deeper inquiry into the nature of the moral condition itself. Is it s moral condition?" and "we are deeply committed to the right and duty of ecclesiastical authority to teach the truth, but not to the presumption that ecclesiastical authority can create truth."

Thomas Kuhn in the **Structure of Scientific Revolution** says that a paradigm both helps us to see and organize data but that it also inhibits and blocks new information. A paradigm in science is a grand theory or model used to direct, guide, test research. At a certain point it outlives its usefulness and a new one is created, often with great resistance and facing outright persecution. Shifts from Aristotle to Newton to Einstein in physics did not take place easily. Looking upon Genesis 1 and 2 as stories about creation rather that actual reports of facts did not come easy and is still resisted by many who think it is literal.

Does time now call for the Church to shift its sexual paradigm, the way it see and organizes data? Is it time to abandon the idea of natural law about sex and contraception? Is it time for the Church to give full opportunity to women, opening up ordination to them? Allowing priests to marry? Declaring homosexuality a genetic imprint and allowing homosexuals full participation in the Church, without the stigma of "sinners"?

I say it is time and to delay longer puts the Church in a position of officially backing evil, the persecution of gays.

Perhaps this is the time to examine the whole concept of sex as it relates to marriage. Can women be free if marriage continues? How? Freedom is the key to individual growth. When inhibitions and restraints are unjustly imposed on segments of society, we do not have a free society and the limiting of such talents inhibits all of us, whether it's voting right's, baseball, jobs, housing, education. It's time to create a new paradigm, a new way of seeing one another and enjoying the diversity of creation.

As late as October, 1994 the Vatican's Congregation for Institutes of Consecrated Life and Societies of Apostolic Life was overseeing an investigation of the homosexuals in the ministry of Father Nugent and Sister Jeannine Gramicle. The charge against them is that their teaching, writing, and speaking about homosexuals is ambiguous, itself an ambiguous charge.

Sister Gramicle and Father Nugent have been conducting seminars and programs aimed at developing understanding about homosexuality. Bishop John M. D'Arcy of Fort Wayne warned all priests and educators not to attend an ecumenically sponsored educational program on sex in his diocese.

The investigative body, headed by Archbishop Maida of Detroit, is still gathering information and conducting hearings. You would assume that is homosexuals are "living in sin," as those Church authorities seem think, they would want someone evangelizing and saving them. Of course part of the mission of Gramicle and Nugent is developing understanding of the problem, a desirable objective, and this too is looked upon as questionable.

It seems that some people cannot accept new data that challenges their formal beliefs and tenets. They reject this data like a heart transplant. When a new, healthy heart starts pumping in a malfunctioning system, the rest of the body frequently is unable to handle this activity and rejects the heart. Strong attempts must be made to persuade the other organs to accept this new organism. If the rest of the body does not accept it the patient dies.

Today the Church is confronted with new data on homosexuality. It is time to examine and use this data. Usury, making money by loaning money, forbidden in the Old Testament in many sections, as: Exodus 22:25, Deuteronomy 23:19, Leviticus 25:37, and Psalm 15:5, has not only been accepted but us practiced by the Vatican. If a person is genetically disposed to same sex preference shouldn't it be normal, natural, and also acceptable to the Church?

CHAPTER 15

THE CIVIL RIGHTS MOVEMENT

OF THE SIXTIES

(AS SEEN IN MUSKEGON, MICHIGAN)

To this point in our interpretation we have observed mostly "ancient history" from the beginning of the Christian Era to the twentieth century. It is now time to discuss what actually led to this writing: the Civil Rights movement of the Sixties. This chapter will be more personal than any of the others, because I, as a Roman Catholic Priest, participated in that movement for several years, and one of my fellow leaders, Dr. James Jackson, D.O., urged me to record these memories. Thus I will write this lengthier chapter in the first person.

All history is interpretation. We tend to think of studying history as studying facts. Any history is a person's or persons' records and comments, usually with huge gaps, many innuendoes, and some or many outright errors. Witness American History to date which omits almost all the contributions of over half of our people - WOMEN! Our history is the record of men, about men, a very limited view and perspective.

My history of civil rights in Muskegon, Michigan from 1962 to 1967 is my view, my interpretation. My writings record some of the events, conversation, responses, results, fears, and more that happened to me and around me, as I, a priest became more and more embroiled in controversy as I identified with actions intended to gain blacks their civil rights.

As a priest I was trained to see the importance of justice and I spent my years of preparation in the Seminary studying not only text books but also familiarizing myself with the social encyclical letter of Pope Leo XIII and Pius XI. I worked among the poor in Washington DC during my free time as a student at Theological College Catholic University of America. I discovered that very few blacks were Catholic and most of them were poor.

I determined to try and work among blacks after I became a priest. In 1960, I learned that the Bishop of Grand Rapids, Allen J. Babcock, was interested in trying to convert blacks to Catholicism. I volunteered for this task and in 1961 I was appointed Director of the Catholic Information Center in Muskegon Heights, Michigan. At this time the Center did not exist but I went to Muskegon to lead an effort to build a center which would be located in the midst of the black population of Muskegon Heights.

Aiding me in this venture, and cooperating to the hilt was Monsignor Albert Kehren, pastor of Sacred Heart Church in Muskegon Heights. Monsignor Kehren was a leader in the community and interested in this project. He had already purchased a site for a building and he invited me to live in his rectory until I got started. He was a gracious host and entirely cooperative. The other priests in the area were mildly interested. Some were worried about black converts. Where would they attend Church and what would be the reactions of other white Catholics?

My plan was to build the Center, begin convert classes, met as many blacks as possible, and have bible school sessions for children. My main action plan was walking in the area, wearing my black suit and roman collar. Soon people would wonder what I was about and I could begin by conversation, a conversation that would lead to instruction, conversion, and incorporation into existing parishes. We did not want to begin a black catholic parish.

In a couple of years I had obtained enough money from the Bishop and the Extension Society, a missionary group, to put up the building and I moved in to begin evangelization. During this time and earlier, the Civil Rights Movements had begun in the South. I paid no attention to the bus-boycotts, sit-ins at lunch counters, the freedom riders, and the entrance into the movement by Martin Luther King.

By 1963 this movement reached Muskegon, Michigan. I attended an Urban League meeting as a member of the board, and at this session I publicly stated that segregated housing was the root of the "Negro problem." Segregated housing led to job discrimination, segregated schools, and the alienation of the Negro community. I said this and received mild applause and some looks of wonder that I would know this, and more, say it.

The next day Doctor James Jackson D.O. called me and said, "I heard you at the Urban League meeting yesterday. Were you serious or were you just talking?" Here was a very blunt opener in what was to lead to friendship that continued and a commitment that led to my ultimately leaving the priesthood. I responded, "I was serious." Jim then said, "All right, we can use you. I'll be calling you later."

In a few days he called and said, "We are forming an action group called *The Council of Equal Opportunity*. We will initially be trying to integrate the work forces in the stores where no blacks are employed: Sears, Penneys, and all the big stores in town, also the loan companies, dairies, and whatever."

I said, "What do you want me to do?" He then scared me by saying, "You will make the phone calls to the manager of the stores to get appointments for us to talk to them about hiring blacks in sales positions." I did not feel comfortable about this but I knew I was committed so I agreed. He told me Dr. Frank Howell DDS, an antique dealer Jim Tate and Rev. Bennett, a black minister, would accompany us on our visits.

The strategy was to ask the managers to hire a qualified black person, possibly supplied by the Urban League, the next time an opening came on their staff. Usually the manager resisted by saying, "You can't tell me how to run this business and I don't like force," we advised him that since blacks shopped in his store ir would be good for them to see some black employees. If he refused, we would put a picket line in front of the store and announce in the black churches to boycott the store unless it cooperated. Since Muskegon was an area of heavy industry it was a strong union town and picket lines would be very effective because most would be fearful of crossing the line. We could in effect, in a very short time, shut down most of the store's business.

When I joined some of the picket lines downtown I got an immediate hostile reaction. Many Catholics were alarmed to see a priest our walking on a picket line. Some of them hated blacks and their prejudices surfaced. I became an enemy to many of these Catholics.

Almost immediately people began writing to the Bishop about the "scandal" I was causing. Soon I received letters from the Bishop cautioning me that what I was doing was "lay-peoples' work." The trouble was that many lay people did not have time or energy for this task and few could risk their jobs because of reprisals. As one of my priest friends explained to the Bishop, :you have to put your money and body where your mouth is."

The Bishop has a diocesan-wide money collection called the Diocesan Development Fund (DDF). He had allocated some of these moneys to me for my building. Now people began threateh9hg to cut off contributions to the DDF because of me. The Bishop became angry at a statement I made, quoting a passage out of the Old Testament, "all thing obey money."

Actually it was true and that is why it was irritating. It took me a while to realize that people go to Church on Sunday to get a good feeling that all is well between them and God and their fellow-man. They do not want the preacher bothering them, making their life uncomfortable. I began to do this as I preached on civil rights, prejudice, poverty, and the need for social justice and action.

I remember some people passing our leaflets on the black Muslims at a suburban church. I never could figure out why, because there were only a handful of black Muslims in the whole area. The leaflet denigrated the Muslims and was false. I read the Muslim paper and studied their teaching. They were good people. I got up in the Church and denounced the leaflet and explained what the Muslims taught. Several people became angry and got up and walked out of the Church during the sermon.

When you preach strong doctrines you repel many but you also attract some. Some of the finest Christians I ever met came to join us in our efforts. Some risked their jobs, reputations, and social acceptance. They saw the righteousness of the cause and they stepped forward. Among these was my future wife Sonja.

On Sundays I usually helped out at a Polish parish in town. The pastor was a bigot and was terrified of the civil rights movement. He told me I could not preach about any of these issues in "his" church. He told me if picketers came to :his" church I would be fired. Usually I couldn't join picketers on Sunday because I was busy. We walked in front of Churches to draw attention to the cause and reach peoples' consciences. Signs were carried that said "What is your pastor doing for civil rights?" "Charity is more than Church," and "Justice for all." As I mentioned earlier people go to Church to get a good feeling and these picketers and signs at the door were bothersome.

The pastor of the Polish Parish said to me, "Do not explain any of this to my people. There could be bloodshed." Actually, they were mostly hardworking people who believed in live and let live. How mistaken he was in predicting bloodshed was shown when two old Polish women approached the Church the Sunday the picketers were there. One asked, "What do the signs say?" The other responded, "Spaghetti dinner at Catholic Central." So much for the inflammatory picketers.

As stated earlier, I had a bible school at the Center but one day a sister of St. Dominic, Lois Lynch, who helped teach, came in and said, "These children are having trouble reading. We should be conducting a remedial reading school here instead if bible school." I immediately okayed this change and we sent a note home with all the children about what we were doing. Attendance grew.

Most of the planning sessions and rallies related to civil rights took place at the Center. I can see how people who contributed money to the Center so that we could convert blacks were upset that some of our efforts went to other mundane causes like civil rights. Even the Bible school became a reading school. We were living in changing and turbulent times and life was sometimes difficult.

I kept hearing certain words again and again during those years. They were words geared to slow down the movement and restrain progress. Some of the words and expressions were: wait, be patient, use caution, takes your tie, never use force, use restraint, love will win in the end. I always believed that time would take care of a lot of problems. I read "Time heals all wounds" and "Time wounds all heals." I learned from Martin Luther King that time is neutral. It does nothing. Time in itself brings no change. We introduce change.

The more I thought about the evils of segregation, the more I realized that these problems of our society were so deeply rooted that only force could change them. When I stated these ideas publicly I was looked upon as a communist and an anarchist. To me it looked like common sense. Which gets back to my idea of history as interpretation.

Along with all the turmoil and grief some funny things happened. A black woman convert of mine came to me stating she wanted her children to attend a parochial school in a largely Italian based parish. I asked her what the problem was and she stated that the pastor told her he wanted the tuition up front. He referred to the situation of Negroes moving into his territory as "a black cloud has come over my parish." It was my opinion that he was at best prejudiced.

At that time (1965) tuition was very low but still a family of twelve children was at stake, and it took all their money for ordinary expenses. I asked, "What is the tuition and how many children will be going to school?. She said "Eight, and the price is twenty-five dollars for the first child, and fifteen dollars for the second and third, and ten dollars for all the other children." I added this up and it came to one hundred and twenty-five dollars.

I happened to have some extra money in the bank, garnered from preaching retreats and giving graduation talks. I said to Mrs. Jenkins, "education costs money and so does entertainment. We can, with this opportunity, help educate your children plus integrate every classroom in the school with one stroke and be amused at the pastor's reaction. So, I will give you a check for one hundred and twenty-five dollars which you take to the bank and cash and get a bank check so the pastor won't know where you got the money. I want it to be a secret.

She agreed and so it was done. In a couple of days I got a phone call form this pastor in which he expressed great surprise. He confessed to me, "John, I will have to give these Negroes credit. I told Mrs. Jenkins I needed one hundred and twenty-five dollars is she wanted her children in the school. I never dreamed she could come up with the money. Now I have to keep my promise and let all those children into my school."

I got another phone call for the same pastor asking about how I managed to validate a marriage of another black couple in his parish. He prided himself on his knowledge of Canon Law, even though he actually knew very little. I found an ancient decree call "O Altitudo" in back of the Canon Law text which stated that if in missionary countries people were uprooted and went to other lands, as in the case of slaves, they could remarry. At the end of the decree stated, it "Wherever similar circumstances apply this decree applies." This loophole was all I needed to validate the marriages of many blacks who were uprooted during the war, moved from the South, and later remarried. If I had proposed this case to the marriage tribunal in Grand Rapids, Michigan, the decision would either be still pending, or denied as preposterous.

In such instances I just used common sense and applied different decrees without consultation. Thus is was that I "solved" many cases. Part of this I learned from a former Army Chaplain, William Zuidema, who said he had found in the army that by the time he got even some of the required paperwork together, people had been transferred, so as soon as he was reasonably certain of the data, he acted on it and validated many Marriages. I began to do the same so it was more than civil rights that caused friction in my life in Church. I was finding bureaucratic lethargy that from my viewing, ended in legalism and kept us from getting on with life and solving real problems instead of paper problems.

Along with this I got into trouble over my attitude about the Bible. I realized that many items in the Bible were written in different literary forms and required interpretation. For instance, I thought that the narration about Noah's Ark was a story, told to tell a truth, namely if you act up and so evil, you will be punished. "Let me tell you a story, not a factual story, but a story to illustrate this."

This made sense to me and to most of the faithful with whom I dealt. It didn't to a Franciscan pastor, in whose parish I was conducting the sophomore retreat of the youth from Catholic Central in Muskegon, Michigan. The pastor stayed in the sacristy as I talked. I could hear his sandals flapping and his rosary beads clanging. He reported what I said about Noah's Ark to the Bishop and I got called on the carpet for this heresy." It reminded me of Galileo who knew he was right and was told by the Pope frankly to "shut up."

This altercation over the Bible, along with my continued fracas over civil rights, led me to think I was in the wrong business. What I thought was true and I was willing to die for, was not the same as what the Bishop, our pastor, and leaders, thought. I has serious doubts now after I had spent twelve years in the Seminary and had been a priest for sixteen years. I was I a form of shock. I will recount more later in this chapter.

I was invited to give talks to various civic groups and organizations. They wanted to drum up excitement at the meetings and they usually had a member who knew me or about me. The usually got more than they bargained for. One of my problems was that I told the truth, I knew too much about the problems and I laid the cards on the table and showed responsibility.

Someone invited me to address the teachers' convention one October and the man specifically said, "Tell these teachers the truth and see if you can rile them up." This type of charge was not usually necessary since it happened anyway. However, I could not resist this challenge. One of the statements I made went like this:

> Since teachers are supposedly leaders in the community and should model the behavior they teach, I assume that they teach equality in the classroom and treat everyone fairly. I would also expect to see them in the forefront of the Civil Rights Movement. Where are they? We don't have any in our group. No one has come forward to join us, march with us, picket with us, or do anything with us. I challenge you now to step forward and declare yourselves as to whose side you are on.

I received mild applause and then the superintendent of schools stood and said, "Our teachers are doing a marvelous job and need no prodding." He received thunderous applause. I was embarrassed, not for myself, but by the outright hypocrisy being used as a cloak. It was merely self-serving and an attempt to escape social responsibility and social action. As the room cleared I lingered to look directly at all who would make eye contact with me. One person did and he came up to the podium when I was all alone.

" Father Sheehy," he remarked, "you are absolutely right and I am ashamed to say that I did not have enough never to stand and take your side. We all live in fear of our superiors, we are afraid to risk tenure, so you were treated so poorly here today and I apologize. I thought you might like to know that secretly many of us agree with you but we do not have the courage to back your cause."

I was the chaplain of the Knights of Columbus Council in Muskegon, Michigan. Msgr. Kehren had arranged this before I became a controversial figure. I decided to challenge them. They referred to themselves as "the strong right are of the Church." They were supposed to be militant Catholics. Of course no one really knew what that meant or entailed. In that day in the sixties, it meant nothing. At a regular meeting, I invited them, about fifty men from all the parishes of the area, to join us in achieving civil rights.

At that time I was not aware that women needed civil rights too or I would have asked them to open their doors to women members. I can see now how I too was blinded about women's issues. However, after I made my special appeal, one of the members rose to rebut me. He said, "You are a celibate, and have no daughters who might be imperiled by this movement, so you can afford to press these issues. We cannot and will not." He sat down to lengthy applause. I was appalled since I thought my celibacy (at that time) was a witness to the strength of my dedication to Christ and his teaching. Now it was being used as a weapon to help squelch the civil rights movement. I responded, "I cannot believe what you have just said to me, a gross insult to your chaplain and the teaching of the Church. I resign as you chaplain." Not a single person came to my cause. I left defeated, chagrined and sad.

It was becoming clear to me that either we didn't do a good job teaching justice to our clergy and members or I must have gotten the message wrong. I found it difficult to face the incongruity between scriptural emphasis on poverty, helping the poor and defenseless, and the official attitude of Church authority and roughly 90% of the lay parishioners. It was pointed out to me again and again that I was acting against Church teaching, especially in my methods. No one approved the concept of force as evidenced in boycotts, picketing, marches, and confrontation. -

I was interviewed by a reporter for The Muskegon Chronicle and he asked me how I thought these social inequities could be remedied. I said, "Through force. Otherwise it will not happen. People like the status quo, they do not like to be told about these problems and hope they will all just go away. We must apply pressure to right our society.

Otherwise there will be revolution." At the time this statement caused uproar in Muskegon. "Priest recommends force."

Statements like this terrify normal mortals. Doctor Jackson said something similar. "Everyone thought we were recommending violence and bloodshed. We were not. We were merely pointing out what would happen if social change did not take place. We were right, as was evidenced by the many riots that have taken place since. The job had still not been done and I predict again that if social change, justice, and equal opportunity do not occur soon, our society will become unmanageable and extreme violence will occur. As poverty, hunger, homelessness, squalor, disease, and drug use increase the final chaotic scene is inevitable.

I always have labored under the mistaken notion that is facts were presented, if the truth were told forcefully enough, people would assent to the data and make adjustments. They don't. It has been demonstrated that 80% of our decisions are based on sentiment, feelings, and beliefs. If you tell people about unemployment, lack of opportunity for the poor and give them data you will hear statements like these:

> I fight poverty, I work.
>
> These people are too lazy to work.
>
> My grandparents, parents and I got up off the ground and made it.
>
> You can't just throw money at problems.

They forget that some of their grandparents got where they did by taking land from the Indians, killing those who resisted, and informing the survivors that they should join us "civilized folks" or perish.

I was asked by the State of Michigan Civil Rights Commission to attend a hearing on racial issues at Muskegon Catholic Central. I always thought that these types of hearing were a waste of time. People gave endless testimony, all was recorded and listened to, taken "under advisement" and then nothing happened.

So, when I went there I was already not in a good mood. I had reached a point where things were really clear to me and I knew when something was going to happen and when it wasn't. Mostly, I knew that I and others in our group had to "make it happen," otherwise nothing would happen. I was convinced that this hearing was a waste of time. Nothing did ever come of it.

However, during my testimony a Negro minister, wearing a roman collar like mine, asked! "What is the Church doing about Civil Rights?" A great question to which I responded "Nothing. And not only that, the hierarchy of the Church tries to keep people like me from doing anything either. Not only will they not do anything, they prevent others, similar to the Pharisees that Jesus said would not enter nor would they allow others to enter."

I didn't know there was a reported from the Associated Press there but it wouldn't have affected what I had said anyway, but it was put on the state wire. This was a Friday and it was published on the State page of the Grand Rapids Press on Sunday. The headline stated, "Priest attacks Bishops." When I saw the headline, I said to myself, "I've got to find out who this priest is and get to meet him. He sounds like a kindred soul." As I read the first paragraph I saw my name as the protagonist. Then I said, "Wow!" Just then the phone rang and be father was on the phone from Grand Rapids. He had never before called me long distance. He said, "I think its too late." And it was.

Several people told my mother that she should be proud of me because I spoke the truth and she passed this on to me She was afraid, like my dad that I was getting into trouble but basically she backed me up. I think my father was terrified.

I was convinced that open housing would lead to a solution and so was Dr. Jackson and Dr. Howell. Dr. Jackson managed to get some property near Mr. Garfield from a person interested in racial justice. Frank Howell couldn't seem to pull it off so he asked me to buy some property in an all white area and then deed it over to him. He supplied the money and I bought the property. How they could trust selling any property to me was beyond my comprehension but the did.

I was so identified with the cause that frequently I spent no time thinking about with whom I was dealing. I was never a political animal. At an NAACP meeting I remonstrated with a black doctor, a physician, not Dr. Jackson, that he was no militant enough. He blurted out "You better watch what you're saying. I've been a Negro a lot longer than you have." He was right about that, regardless of our ages, but I considered it a compliment that he thought I was black. I guess I was spiritually and mentally black and the sufficed for him.

A few time a year I would go to different parishes and preach so I could raise some money to run the Center. The Bishop allowed me these "Missionary collections." Father Tom Schiller was a friend of mine and he invited me to preach in his parish and one time I also went to Father Joe Battersby's parish in Empire. After I finished my appeal, Father Joe, who was a real character, stepped to the microphone because he didn't think I had sufficiently pressed the issue of my financial needs. Father Joe said, "Father Sheehy had sold his body and soul for the American Negro and you better dig down and contribute mightily to his cause or you will all feel guilty." The collection was indeed one of the best.

Of course many people who saw me at these fund-raisers thought I was a humor-filled Irishman, quite harmless on the circuit. I was that, but when I was engaged in civil rights, people thought me an anarchist rabble rouse.

So it was that shortly after I came to Muskegon, the leadership at Catholic Central thought ir best I not teach there because I taught a course in "religionless Christianity," which stressed not studying catechism or religion, but working in the community. My students went to class one hour a week and worked in the community four hours. This was their religion class. Some of them helped in the remedial reading school at the Center. Most students, who were seniors, and had the option on this class declined and it ultimately was deemed too controversial by the administration.

To return to the housing issue, at a certain point we decided to attack the Board of Realtors. We asked them to meet with the Council of Equal Opportunity, and they agreed. A smoother group that was into denial we had never met. They claimed all housing was on the open market and any qualified black could by just like anyone else.

This was a joke then and it still is more than 25 years later. Its better, but its still there. Michael Jordan was having trouble recently in Long Beach, Michigan City, Indiana.

I suggested that they issue a statement like this to all clients. We refuse to list any property that will not be sold on the open market to any qualified buyer, regardless of race, color, or creed. They refused on the grounds that it would impinge on others' rights and liberties'. They said there was no problem. There was no good way for us to deal with these people. Picketing would be a waste of time. There were too many of them and their sales took place everywhere.

We formed our own reality company, Home Equity Inc. We had two Catholic lawyers who backed us. They helped us on the legal angles. They did all they could to help. They were part of a small minority of Catholic, most of the local Catholic clergy did not actively back the process and it was a scary business. People were being killed in the South, trying to get voting rights. The Klan was still powerful and incited murder of those who got out of line. Its no wonder people were intimidated and since they received no encouragement from the hierarchy of the church, many took the east way out.

I planned to go to Mississippi on one of my vacations and help register voters in the South. Somehow the local Bishop form the area obtained a list of priest volunteers and wrote to my Bishop, Allen J. Babcock, to request that he keep me from coming. I received a copy of the Bishop's letter and a request from my Bishop to comply with his wishes. At the time I convinced myself it was the right thing to follow what the Bishop asked.

Now I think I was terrified to go there for fear I would be killed. Many other from the North were killed and I would have been a target. I was actually relieved when I got that letter and I wrote and advised the voter registers I was not coming.

As I write this today I feel I should have gone. I eventually disobeyed the Bishop anyway when he forbade me to picket. For a while I complied and then I was shamed by the hypocrisy of this stance. At a priest's ordination he places his hand in the Bishop's and pledges obedience to him and to his successors. Do you obey, when in your heart, the Bishop is wrong? Many do and this is still going on, especially when Rome speaks. Even today, liberation theology, which option states that the poor should guide our interpretation of the scriptures, is looked upon critically by the Vatican and most bishops. Do you wonder how we could get so far away form Jesus who said, Blessed are the Poor" and "the Son of Man had nowhere to lay his head." Now looking at anything favoring the poor is questionable and heretical? If you read Leonardo Boff from South America you would find nothing objectionable that I can divine and yet the Vatican has silenced him. He is a liberation theologian.

Many of my friends were relieved when I told them I wasn't going to register voters, especially the woman I eventually married. Sonja Rae Richards, one of the first activists in the movement, who brought all the children to the picket line. This lead to her oldest son's future career in t he army being question because his name was on an FBI list for picketing. The civil and clerical lists of suspicious characters include all rebellious types even children.

Civil rights also involved others than Roman Catholic clergy. At Dr. Jackson's behest we asked several Negro ministers to accompany us. Some like Rev. Bennett, backed us to the utmost, allowed us to talk at their Churches, and espoused our ideas. However, the fact that some business people in the community made charitable donation to black Churches and to come of the ministers, was used to divide us. The establishment would use anything to maintain the status quo, including intimidation, bribery and blackmail.

One visit was scheduled to Sanitary Dairy and this time only a black minister and I could be free to make the call. By this time I was thoroughly trained by watching Dr. Jackson operate so I didn't see this as a problem.

I picked up the Reverend and we went to the Dairy. As we entered the room I noticed a man with a yellow legal pad sitting near the owner. The owner did not introduce us to him after I told him who we were. When I sat down I inquired of the unidentified man, "So you happen to be an attorney?' He said, "yes." I then said, "good. Write down everything I say because it will all be legal and must be done if we wish to save our society." He looked scared and responded, "I will."

At that time Sanitary Dairy had about 100 employees and none of them was black. I advised the owner when his next job opened, we wanted him to hire a qualified black. The attorney was busy taking notes and I was glad. At a certain point the owner inquired again of the pastor's name and what church he pastored. When he got his information he reached in a desk drawer and extracted a few pages of typewritten material. He scanned it and then remarked, "Ah, I see we supplied free milk for the children attending your Bible School and for a major parish fund-raising dinner." The minister cowered and said, "Yes you did and we are extremely grateful and look forward to other such donations."

I was appalled and chagrined. This attempt at blackmail was not going to work. I raised my voice with, "Put that list back in the drawer and if you bring anything like that up again I'm really going to get angry." I turned to the lawyer and said "Write that down." He said

"Yes, sir" and began to write. Then I told the owner we were here to talk about jobs and nothing else and we got back on the subject.

As members of Home Equity we were trying to integrate neighborhoods and we went to various black Churches to discuss this idea. Of course this endangered some of the black pastors because they felt they might lose some of their wealthy parishioners. One of them got up after we left and told people to ignore us. I spoke to Dr. Jackson about this and told him we should get after these ministers. He said no, they are no the enemy, the white establishment is. I thought this over and then agreed with him and this same attitude came through years later when my wife cautioned members of NOPW never denigrate women who disagreed with NOW's policy. She said, "Women are not the enemy, White males are."

One time, after we left a furniture store, Dr. Jackson told me to go back in and extract our black minister companion. I asked Jim why he didn't do it and he informed me he did not want to alienate the minister. I said, "What is he doing in there?" Jim said the owner was probably offering a chair or something for his rectory - another attempt at bribery. I went back and found the owner talking confidentially to the minister. I advised him that we were finished and he should now leave. He did not want to comply but I forced him. I realized again what a smart man Jim Jackson was.

Not only did the Catholic church not officially back or foster the civil rights movement but other Churches also mostly did nothing or else backed the establishment. An Episcopal priest friend of mine, Bob Cunningham, was pastor of an Anglican parish in the suburbs. He and his wife Mary were socially conscious and Bob openly advocated civil rights and stood so strongly on issues that it irritated some rich member of his parish and they started an uproar among the members. Finally his Bishop came and tried to quell the storm. Some of Bob's Parishioners were ardent advocates of civil rights and took his side but others were strongly against him. Once again money played a role. Some of the wealthy people threatened to boycott the parish and withhold funds. This storm of protest and the failure of the Bishop to back Bob and Mary led him to finally leave the active ministry as it did me.

Eventually the white power structure saw that we meant business and they began actively to diffuse our movement. They asked for meetings with us, the Council of Equal Opportunity, the NAACP, and the Urban League. We agreed to the meeting and they said they wanted to form The Committee of a Hundred, composed of key community leaders, businessmen, pastors, and some of us, to begin a community wide effort to obtain jobs and break segregation.

I was suspicious of this from the start and recommended to our group that we not join. Also I said, "They will try to take credit for all we have done." A fellow member of our group said to me, "If all you want is credit you better get out." Already divisions had set in and things were never the same. We agreed to give up calling on merchants, picketing and rallies, in exchange for what the Committee would do. They began endless talks and meeting. They coopted us and practically destroyed us.

Shortly thereafter the Black Power movement started and this further diminished our drive. I went to a black Church to attend what I thought was a civil rights meeting and I was told, "You are not black and you cannot attend. Haven't you heard of black power?" Actually I had not and no one told me or cushioned this blow.

I walked out of that Church feeling totally rejected and dejected. I had antagonized most of the people in Muskegon fighting for Civil Rights and now I wasn't welcome among blacks.

Then I went to see my friend Jim Jackson and asked him what to do. He said I had to make a decision about the Church. The Bishop was getting ready to transfer me. I was disillusioned with the Church. Jim said, "Why don't you go to school and get a negotiable degree?" This sounded like a great idea to me. I had a Bachelor of Philosophy degree and teaching degree in Theology. I wrote to the Bishop and asked to go to Notre Dame to get a degree in Sociology. He readily gave permission and agreed to pay all the bills. What a great way to compromise and solve a problem for both of us.

I went to Notre Dame in 1967 and received a Mater's degree. I decided to get married and took a job working for Bethlehem Steel Corp.

Before I formally let I discovered again my incompatibility with Church work. I went to a parish at Interlochan near Traverse City, Michigan to help out another priest. It was the Sunday after the Democratic Convention in Chicago, 1968. I mentioned in my sermon that we should be listening to the young people and not beating them over the head. I stated that I thought the Chicago police had not handled the situation well. When I finished my remarks, I asked the congregation for feedback. An elderly woman in the front pew stood up and said, "I think the Chicago police did just fine and you are entirely wrong." The whole Church broke into spontaneous applause.

I couldn't believe this because one could rarely get a whole church of Catholics to join anything. I felt afraid because I could see open hostility on their faces. Then a man in the back started hollering "Who are you to tell us what the answers are? You don't know anything about it." Others shouted agreement with him. I really began to feel fear. I took a deep breath and responded, "I don't really know the answers I am a sociologist from Notre Dame, and I came here to pose some questions and provoke some discussion. I see I have done that so now I will resume the Mass."

I returned to the altar feeling afraid. Here I was an ordained leader of the flock, afraid for my life at the hands of the flock. I was not imagining or exaggerating because after the Mass the usher came and said "I was trying to figure how to get you out of here alive if they came after you." It was them I realized that my messages would be too strong for most congregations and I knew I was on the right path. I had to figure out what to do to find another vocation.

Years later a friend of mind, a former priest, half-heartedly suggested that I preach in his Church, a rich upper-class lily-white Protestant group. I said, "Do you want to close this place? I can do it for you in one Sunday."

The pastor who fired me because of picketers who came to his parish was so isolated from the community that he became terrified of the whole civil rights movement and of blacks in general. He told me he kept a loaded shotgun by the front door of the rectory in case, he said, "the jungle bunnies" come to the rectory to use force and violence.

No one recommended the use of violence, although the Black Muslims used stronger language than we did. Malcolm X said, "If you're trying to start a revolution you don't go out in the street and start singing. You start swinging." I doubt very much at that time, or even now, that any blacks would become so disturbed they would attack a Church or a priest's house. If our society continues to separate the rich from the poor more and more, and cause widespread depravation, then hostility and anger will come, form people within and outside the United States.

The Bishop, at a meeting of the pastors of the Muskegon area basically advised the priest to stay out of the civil rights area (this was more for my benefit since none of them had any intention to getting in it), but to preach to the people about these problems, since they were "lay-people's problems?"

I had lost all tolerance with these racists and knew that none of them even understood the problems, so how could they instruct the people. Actually, seminary training spent no time on social problems or on justice in terms of the poor, or especially about segregation. The seminarians who were interested in these questions were looked upon as radical troublemakers and weirdoes. Small wonder the priests knew nothing about it and didn't want to bother with it.

At this meeting I pointed out to the Bishop that the pastor of the parish I assisted on Sunday, the one with the shotgun at the door had forbidden me to preach on these issues. Everyone looked at me as a leper. Jesus said, "the truth shall make you free." The question that Pilate asked was a good one: "What is truth?" I thought I possessed the truth about the poor, the problem, and some solutions. Very few of my fellow priests agreed with me, except a few younger contemporaries, some of whom even came and picketed in my place after the Bishop had forbidden me to picket.

I was frequently called on the carpet by the Bishop on subjects related to the Scripture and civil rights. One time I was really surprised because it had no foundation. The Bishop asked me "Why did you tell children not to go to school on Martin Luther King's birthday?" This really dumbfounded me because I considered King too passive at that time and had no idea of the impact he was making in the South or what influence he had on the Kennedys and Johnson.

I responded, "Why would I tell someone else's children what to do about going to school." The Bishop still thinking the report was correct contented, "That's my question. Why did you?" I became indignant and informed him I had done no such thing. I demanded to know who told him this lie. He responded, "I came to Grand Rapids to answer a false charge and I have a right to know my accuser."

He then told me it was an old friend of mine who had befriended me. I was crushed and I went straight back to Muskegon to find out what he would say. When I confronted him he denied it so I said, "The Bishop is in his office. Call him and tell him it wasn't you, otherwise you are lying to me." He sheepishly said, "No." I knew he had done this to try and hinder my work. I don't know why. Years later I thought about this and decided it might have been because I cut him out of the loop of information about what we were doing, our plans, our goals. He probably thought, as dean, he had lost control. He had.

I told him I was severing relations with him until he apologized. Several years later his sister wrote to me from Saginaw, Michigan and advised me her brother, this particular priest, was dying and had expressed sorrow to her about what happened between us. I wrote him a letter to the hospital and told him I forgave him and would stop in and see him the next time I came to Grand Rapids. I was in school at Notre Dame at the time. A few days later he died and at least this partial reconciliation took place.

The Civil Rights Movement helped me make some wonderful friends, many of whom I still see and continue dialogues, but it forced a chasm between me and many others, especially the clergy and the Bishop. Of course my problems with the Bishop were more than just social justice. There was a major rift on Biblical interpretation and by this time I had fallen in love with my wife and had decided to leave the ministry and get married.

The Black Power Movement which stressed black responsibility and leadership basically ended my participation in the quest for Civil Rights. At that time I didn't see the connection between Negro rights and women's rights. I thought white women were free. Of course at that time I thought I was free.

By the time the Civil Rights Movement ended I was ready to move on to my Sociology degree. I realized that I also had been a captive of ancient ideas. I didn't realize the Church was a gigantic bureaucracy, the embodiment and keeper of patriarchy. I just thought it too bad the Roman Catholic Church did not openly support Civil Rights.

When I began to write this chapter it dawned on me that the Church has had a history of not backing these rights and frequently, openly fought against them in regard to so called heretics, homosexuals, slaves, Indians, blacks, colonists, and most of all women. I don't think anyone has written a history of the Church from the perspective of civil rights and I believe that my treatment could open the eyes of "truth-seekers."

I my concluding chapters I will recount what I think the Church can and should do. I believe if the Church does not get on the side of the poor, women, and the downtrodden, it will perish. You might ask "What good is it anyway?"

CHAPTER 16

WHAT IS THE MAJOR PROBLEM CAUSED BY THE DENIAL OF HUMAN RIGHTS?

Throughout these pages we have seen the consistent and thorough denial of civil and human rights by Churches. On the face of it the average person would be led to believe the opposite. The Churches preach love and forgiveness, openness to others, the evils of prejudice. However, over the years many institutions seem to get away from their initial purposes and missions.

Today, many people criticize their doctors and dentists as being uncaring and only interested in money. For years people have said about doctors, who were usually male, "He has a poor bedside manner." Now you find it difficult to get a doctor to the bedside at all. Others say they never got good care in a hospital. One doctor told me, "The two worse places to be for your health is the doctor's office and the hospital."

We fine the same criticism leveled against attorneys, bankers, politicians and the groups we are mainly concerned with - Churchmen. Once again the reference is to males because almost all Churches are dominated by males.

What seems to happen is that over the years bad social and individual habits creep into organizations and bureaucracies. Once this malaise sets in, you even hear justification for bad behavior by the leaders as, "Wait until you're here awhile and you'll get used to it. Relax. Join the crowd."

Soon these organizations seem more bent on maintaining themselves and their power positions than they are in their missions. People then begin to equate their true mission with maintaining the status quo, defined by one person as, ":the mess we is in."

So, for example, if a Church refuses to admit that women are fully human and therefore cannot assume leadership functions in the Church, then anyone advancing the idea of, say women and ordination, is dangerous and a heretic. Such a person needs to be suppressed.

The Churches, Catholic and Protestant, have done this almost since they began. They are still doing so, to women, gays, and even the poor. Of course most of the poor are women and children.

Not only do we have the denial of full human rights to women, itself a heinous crime but presently, all around the globe, women are persecuted, raped, murdered by their spouses, and mutilated. In Africa, and elsewhere, females are regularly mutilated by the practice of clitordectomy. The unspeakable tearing, cutting and destroying parts of the female genitalia must stop. Not only does it ruin women's bodies, after killing them, it ruins their souls, and extinguishes the inner spirit and all self-esteem. The church has not taken a stand on this. The <u>Pope says nothing.</u>

This type of extreme violence toward women is replicated in 'war crimes', as recently in Bosnia, slavery, footbinding, suttee, and the world wide continued oppression of women.

More subtle is the cultural colonization of women which is so woven into the fabric of society that women themselves do not see their oppression. Nor do women see how society automatically lowers their self-esteem so that even successful worldly women suffer psychologically. Women continually discount themselves and cannot seem to receive even compliments favorably.

Women's work, praised to the sky in sermons and speeches is valued at nothing in the gross national product. Women themselves have said in interview thousands of times, "I'm just a housewife."

Women are know as somebody's wife or mother. The system, fed and fostered by the Churches, keeps women in a certain defined space and grinds them down unobtrusively.

When girls reach teenage years they already have been well schooled in how different they are, and the changes in their bodies give them evidence of this. Boys start to look upon them as prey and girls are torn between attracting the attention of boys and men and protecting themselves from unwanted advances, date rape and assault.

At this time they learn that most Churches will not recognize them as equal to men. Eve led Adam into sin. Women lead men into sin. For years women sore hats and veils in Church because Paul said, "as a sign of subjection and respect for angels".

The Catholic Church teaches the inferiority of women by forbidding them to become priests and in many parishes they cannot even approach the altar as servers. They can do the laundry and cleaning, make the vestments and bake the bread but they cannot preach or consecrate. That is men's work. One woman said to be about celibacy, "the Church teaches the inferiority of women by saying priests can't marry us."

All civilized countries build shelters for women to protect them form men who have beaten and abused them. Why is this necessary in our so-called civilized world? This evident symptom points to the subjugation of women. For years men were encouraged by Church authorities to punish their wives even with a stick as long as it was not larger than a thumb. Many Churches still advocate the physical beating of children as "spare the rod, spoil the child.'

The subjugation of women and the rule of patriarchy have inflicted untold wounds on humanity. It takes a tremendous amount of energy on the part of the oppressor to keep women in subjection and it prevents the development of half the human race. It also hinders the development of males because it cuts down on competition.

We could become grandiose in our description of utopia and how it would operate. Actually, we don't really know what we want. It would have to evolve out of the emotions, thought and expression of all of humankind. This will not happen until everyone has food, clothing, and shelter to start with. Then we need to educate all of humanity with equal opportunity. We waste countless money building armaments to wage war. As I write this in 1996 there are 71 wars or states of war like - situations going on in the world. We need to abolish war and yet we don't seem able to do it. Women hate war, are the primary victims, as also are children, especially since World War II when we began to develop new methods of destruction to wipe out whole cities. The President of the United States even bragged on TV how we shut down the power, water and transportation of Baghdad, thus harming women and children.

Ethics is the study of the underlying assumptions used to determine what is right and wrong. Most of these systems of ethics have been created by men. This may be one of the roots of our modern problems because men are deciding morality and then making laws about it. A practical application of this can been seen in that most pro-choice foes are men and they are making the laws about women's bodies.

Ethics is a practical application of philosophy, a branch of knowledge almost unknown to most of the world and many even look on it as a waste of time. Yet, philosophy deals with definition, truths, how knowledge is processed and is the analysis and synthesis of our experience. It is metaphysics that focuses on being, who are we? Thus, if I can tell a woman she is anything I can then tell her what she should do. I proceed, without a pause or thought from the definition of being to ethics. Very few people think about this or see the serious ramifications and results.

So the would of religion and politics has defined women as inferior creatures, although beautiful like flowers, who are on earth to serve, please, sexually satisfy and work for men. They are defined as: childbearers, homemakers, lovers, cooks, cleaners, and complainers. We must face it, if we define women this way and keep them subject we will never be able to build a society that can evolve ideally.

The ideal society would be one in which each person had equal opportunity and choice. Of course there is no actual possibility for complete equal opportunity. Our own genes, environment and even our desires limit us. But we all need a chance. A plant will not develop if someone is stepping on it, crushing it, providing no nourishment or water, no sunshine. Plants, like people, need a chance to grow, and even given equal opportunity, will all turn out unique individuals.

So, we should provide everyone with a chance to be fully human, fully alive. Some might not choose to develop their talents, to help humanity, to live and unite for the common good. Perhaps there will always be some weak or evil people. We don't know because we haven't tried to eliminate evil or weakness.

The ideal society would be one in which we maximize creativity, we would give every person born the opportunity to grow, develop, and become creative so that each person can take care of herself. No one would be dependent except children, the old or the severely handicapped. The fact that we are all different could be seen as a strength rather than a threat. The eye needs the brain and the brain needs the hand. Why are we presently so threatened by diversity and cultural nuances?

The major problem, the root cause of most other problems, is our stress in gender differences. Men and women are different sexually of course, and their hormonal systems differ, and maybe even the brains are wired differently. Yet we all came from an egg and a sperm and initially we are all females. We are more alike than we are different. Still we are raised so divergently, mostly in the beginning, by females, with little input from males so we evolve as disparate characters who cannot communicate or live in amity.

Men are taught to be macho, logical, with suppressed feelings and with a fear of intimacy. When a man marries he is looking for a sexual companion, housekeeper, mother to him and to the children, the complete caretaker. A woman who marries expects a companion she can talk to, share work with, love her devotedly, comfort her, be aware of her feelings, in a word - a partner.

At the altar, as they say their vows the male and female are actually pledging two different realities even if they say the same words.

We are raised to not understand one another. As women age and their children leave they become more and more disoriented. If they work for money outside the home they are expected to still take major care of the children and the home. Gradually they become depressed from repressed anger. They suffer from underdeveloped talents and lack of goals.

Men then start to look for a younger more docile, affectionate and sexy companion. His wife ceases to be his mother and sexual servant. The root of this problem is the subjection and unequal treatment of women. To maintain this cultural and now dangerous practice taken a great deal of energy, force and even violence. It is not only ineffective, it is destroying all of us.

Men themselves are suffering terribly under his system. Half their emotions are shut down by training and the culture. Men feel inadequate around women, don't know how to talk to them and fear intimacy. A woman can terrify a man if she says, "I want to get close to you." Unless she means sex and even that initiative might cause fear.

So we see that the Church and other major institutions of society have through patriarchy caused great harm not only to females but all humans and the world itself. No one can wash his or her hands of this issue, look the other way. It will not go away.

It is said "If you're not part of the solution you're part of the problem." In this case, since our focus is primarily on the Church, the Church holds a key to solving the problem and it is the problem. Can it shake itself of this lethargy, examine its practices or is it so into preservation and maintenance that is will again turn its energy into suppression? Perhaps its own survival is at stake. It could become an outmoded institution and die.

CHAPTER 17

WHAT CAN THE CHURCHES DO TO FURTHER HUMAN RIGHTS? WILL THEY?

To reiterate, many of the Christian Churches, along with other religious groups, claim to posses the truth. Although Eastern Religions like the Hindu say there are many paths and do not insist that others follow their path, the Western Churches insist that their way is the right and frequently the only way.

They feel that their job is to transmit these truths to others, and if these truths have been solidified into laws, say the Ten Commandments, then the Church must assure obedience.

However, Church attendees worship for various personal reasons and sometimes are in conflict with Church leaders. This leads to an inconsistency that makes the implementations of programs, even Christian Charity, a wavering uncertain process.

For example, in the United States today (1997) most Roman Catholics do not follow the reaching of the Church on birth control. The Church teaches that no interference in the attempt of the male sperm to penetrate a female egg is tolerated. Yet, more then 80% of American Catholics think a decision on this is private. Because of the strong pro-life stance of the Catholic hierarchy many Roman Catholics find themselves allied with fundamentalists and other right-wing groups that will do anything, including murder, bombing, destruction of property to stop abortions. These two major strains produced by divergent attitudes on contraception and abortion make it difficult for the Catholic Church to function unilaterally as it has for many centuries. This can be compared to the Union Movement, which can no longer control how its members vote. They cannot deliver a union vote.

Today (1997) many Roman Catholics, traditional Democrats, have joined forces with the Republican Party whose far right sections expouse their pro-life cause. However, they soon find themselves in a dilemma how to solve the problem of helping the poor and socially deprived, a group the far-right claims results from sloth as evidenced by the by the bumper-sticker: "I Fight Poverty. I work."

The Catholic Church, laboring with many programs to feed the hungry and shelter the homeless, finds itself in danger of losing funds because of the legislative aims of some the same groups that agree with its pro-life stance. Church leaders and followers suffer sever strain over these divergent pulls and they cannot seem to get on track. They don't seem able to answer the question: whose side are you on?

We have not answered two important questions. What is human life? When does it begin? Without answering these questions we have a large segment of the population in favor of even a constitutional amendment to outlaw abortion. With all the emphasis on fetuses we cannot seem to get to how to feed the starving, house the homeless protect women from rapists and batters!

Other problems plague the Catholic Church. (Similar difficulties beset other Church groups, including Jews and Moslems). The Catholic Bishops are at a loss how to control Theologians and Ethics teachers at major Catholic Universities. This strain is worldwide. Pope John Paul II is a strict constructist trying to preserve the Church in a form and mode of long gone eras. He recently (February 1996) announced that Liberation Theology is dead and gone. This wishful thinking shows how far out of contact he is with reality.

Liberation Theology, which stresses that the Scriptures and modern ecclesial life should always favor "an option for the poor" is far from dead. In reading the Old Testament prophets and the words of Jesus as quoted in the New Testament it would appear fairly obvious that not only is this type of interpretation not dangerous but actually called for and highly recommended.

Because some Liberation Theologians have preached a unity of Marxism and practiced Christianity which was actually followed in the early Church (see Acts 4:32-35) and joined it to their theology, they have terrified the Pope's advisory council, the Curia, and the Pope himself. Therefore they cannot see the importance of small Christian communities among the poor. Instead the hierarchy frequently finds itself aligned with the wealthy. How then will the Church ever help obtain human rights for the women, minorities and the poor of the world? Its main goal seems to be maintenance of poor values, structures, and "truths".

Anyone who has worked in a large organization and even in some small ones realizes the problem of dealing with inertia. Many can see new and better ways of doing things more efficiently and effectively but are turned away quickly with! "This is the way we've always done it. If it isn't broke don't fix it. Don't rock the boat etc." Ironically you can't ever eliminate excessive paper work without presenting another sheet of paper telling how and why you want to eliminate paper work.

Bureaucracy in itself impedes progress. For three centuries the Church was persecuted wherever it went. There was very little bureaucracy to start with but once Constantine and his successors made the Church the official religion of the Roman Empire the Church quickly took steps to maintain itself, perpetuate its control, regulate with rules and procedures. The Church set itself up like imperial Rome and has continued in this mode to the present.

This monstrous bureaucracy has aided the Church in preserving itself but it has also blocked the Church in its true mission. The hierarchy of the Church is chosen for its conservatism, probably since the Council of Trent[12] (1545-1563). The Pope regularly appoints bishops and Cardinals who so his will and so not "rock the boat of Peter." For centuries this worked but not the modern age had caught up with its intransigence and the whole structure is shaking.

Thomas Kuhn in his book The Structure of Scientific Revolutions outlines the importance of paradigms. He says that a paradigm is a grand model used to look at the world in a certain manner. He cites the example of paradigms in science. For years the Book of Genesis was the scientific paradigm with which to view the world. These paradigms were succeeded by the changes of Einstein and quantum physics. Now the world would look different when viewed through a different glass, a new approach, a workable paradigm.

The Church itself is an ancient paradigm the evolved out of the practices of the early Christianity and finally became solidified as a state religion. So much was it like the Holy Roman Empire that it became the Roman Catholic Church. It worked so well as a monarchy with its hierarchy of Nobles, Bishops, Cardinals, Monsignors, and Curia. It had ambassadors' worldwide and tries to control any activities of secular states that might infringe on its rights.

The Catholic Church tried to adapt itself to the modern world when the great pope John XXIII called the Second Vatican Council. Great strides were made but fear crept in and the forces of conservation took over which culminated in the election of the ultra reactionary from conservative Poland John Paul II. He has spent his whole papacy traveling and receiving acclaim and tightening the reins on any and all signs of change or evolution. It seems that the Catholic Church is not going to change its paradigm.

Can the Church, Catholic or Protestant correct the present neglect of human rights? They practice a worldwide subjugation of women, sometimes unobserved, often blatant. Many deny rights to minorities, neglect the needy, ignore starving and sick children, persecute gays, and promote overpopulation and war. The Church needs to put its full power into eliminating sexism, racism and homophobia and teach its

---

[12] This council spanning 18 years and 3 Papal reigns was called to reform the Church before the Reformation of Luther (1520) went any further. It reestablished Catholic teaching, moral practice, common law and Church governance.

people that controlling population growth and disease is not only acceptable but mandatory.

Further conflicts keep the Church from moving in the direction of human rights. In the United States today (1996) the Roman Catholic Bishops are aware that large number of their on-duty priests are no longer practicing celibacy. A priest formerly had to leave the active ministry if he wanted to get married or has sex. Not now. As long as no one raises a fuss, and more Catholics don't care, nothing is done. Why? Because the American Catholic Bishops are short of clergy and they are afraid to confront the Pope and tell him that celibacy must be eliminated and the ordination of women must be allowed to qualified females who prove themselves worthy of ordination.

Instead of dealing with this issue the Catholic Church is stuck on abortion, sex and preventing the changes called for by Vatican Council II. Not only has reform stopped, but also all efforts are marshaled to maintain the status quo.

The early followers of Christ had practically no organization. They first met in the synagogues since they were Jews. When many Jews would not accept Jesus as the Messiah who had risen from the dead, they began to meet on Sundays for "The breaking of the bread", the Eucharist. They met in each other's homes. Later they began to have priests, deacons, and bishops. Soon doctrinal differences arose, practices of diet caused confusion and then came division, sects and name calling.

Jesus said, "By this shall all men know that you are my disciples because you love one another." It would seem that this, the essence of Christianity and almost all world religions, could untie all in a common goal and no one would object to the expression of human love. They could then concentrate their efforts on solving world problems and all would be free from subjugation, persecution and war.

I suggest as a started the present pope or his successor should begin by appointing as many female cardinals[13] as there are males and then reorganize the curia and let them participate in the election of a new pope. The old one could resign and be reelected if the majority so

---

[13] Cardinal, as and-derived from the Latin cardo meaning hinge, is a key persa in the reading of the _____ Church and often occupies a key position locally, say as Arch Bishop of New York. The pope could appoint women cardinals even if they were not yet ordained.

desire. This will immediately create an open Church with a new look to the future.

This action would present a model to other institutions like government, the military, universities and corporations that would be encouraged to give equality to women. For several thousand years we have had practically no input from women in positions of power. We need their input, ideas, and feelings.

Will anything happen? I say NO. Several times (3) I made contact with Church authorities in Chicago and Gary to see if I could get them working on the problems of racism in the United States. We have made little or no progress since the civil rights days of the Sixties. Instead we see the emergence of militant groups, neo-nazis, and the Klan. I could not get any action from the Church authorities. The Church instead concentrates its efforts on meaningless meetings, issuing mission statements, brochures and fighting pro-choice politicians.

Actually the Church's attitude toward abortion rights comes under the larger attitude towards women. Abortion is a phony issue because it concentrates on the woman. No one is really "for abortion".

Abortions, except for the 20% caused naturally, are due to unwanted pregnancies. In this day and age abortion should be totally unnecessary except to protect a woman's life or to remove a dead fetus. If you look at it carefully you will discern that males cause unwanted pregnancies. Yet the legislatures and Churches continually harass females about this problem. It is part of an ancient procedure of blaming the woman.

The Church, Catholic, Protestant, Muslin, or any organized religion first must renounce patriarchy as an outmoded and presently inept way of running the universe. Until the U.S. government forced Universities to give equal rights to women in sports we had practically no women athletes. Now the women of the U.S. dominate whole segments of the Olympics. The civil rights movement of the Sixties forced some of these issues and brought about change - needed change.

Fredrick Douglas, the great Black emancipator said, "the limits of tyrants are proscribed by the endurance of those who they suppress." As long as women support institutions like the Church that enslave and suppress them the Church will continue to curtail human rights. The women are the working, supportive and economic backbone of the

Church. When they withdraw their attendance and their money maybe the hierarchy will listen.

The males of our society, and I include myself, have been raised to be male chauvinists and it is so deeply engrained in the system that it will be hard to eradicate. Perhaps the rest of the problems we face would diminish or die if we kept from oppressing, battering and subjugating women.

Whose side is the Church on in this issue and other Civil Rights issues? For an alcoholic to get cured he must first admit he's got a problem. Does the Church have a problem here? I have made it clear that the Church has systematically been suppressing human rights almost from the beginning. Is it not time to admit it, condemn it and forsake it?

Pope John Paul II said he was going to Mount Sinai to confess the sins of the Church in the year 2000. The number one sin of the Church of the oppression of women.

Pope John XXIII took a terrible phrase "let us pray for the perfidious Jews", from the Good Friday Liturgy, by a simple order. The present Pope can eliminate Patriarchy in the Church with an order. The lingering effects will not go away immediately but the disease will be checked and the healing can begin.

CHAPTER 18

SUMMARY AND EPILOGUE

THE CHURCH - AN OUT MODED PARADIGM

A paradigm is a model used in grammar to show how language functions in a given system. It is also used by scientists to direct their research and study so that everyone is on the same page. A paradigm is a theory that has been canonized and accepted in a given discipline.

For example, prior to Gaiileo, Copernicus and Newton, the explanation of the world was based on Genesis 1 and 2. Because Church authorities held to this paradigm they were exceedingly threatened and silenced Gaiileo. Recently the Roman Catholic Church formally stated it was wrong. Sometimes it takes centuries to accept a new paradigm, even if the old one is no longer useful or explanatory.

It took a long time for Newton's laws of physics to be supplemented by Einstein's theory of relativity and quantum physics. The new paradigm in science is, we are uncertain and deal with approximations and probabilities.

The Church (Roman Catholic and all other models of this institution) is an outmoded paradigm, which went through several serious modifications and then became frozen and remains frozen. Church authorities are similar to Chinese leaders who can see the handwriting on the wall and dig in with all their might.

If you read the first writings of the Christian Church, as I Thessalonians, you see a preoccupation with the Second Coming of Christ. When Christ failed to appear the paradigm shifted. Paul begins to argue about salvation in Romans and Galatians. A fully developed Christology appears in Colossians and Phillipians.

The first Gospel, Mark, emphasizes Jesus as a spirit possessed healer of those demon-possessed. There is no mention of the infancy of Jesus, which appears in later Gospels, as Luke and Matthew, which by the way are significantly different. Who Jesus is or was changes even more in John, where He now is the eternal Word, born before all time. The paradigm of who Jesus is or was shifts, has shifted and will shift. Today, many women see Jesus as a feminist.

However, once a hierarchy was established, as we see happening in the later writings, I and II Timothy and Titus, the Church began to solidify itself into a permanent pattern (up till now) where certain ordained ministers preside, legislate and rule. They begin to lay down dogmas, rituals, scriptures, and interpretations of the scriptures and the right to control the future by picking their successors.

This solidification achieved permanence when the Church modeled itself on the Roman Empire with a central ruler in Rome, the Pope, the local rulers, subject to Rome, the Bishops who rule over priests and ordinary people in their area. They first were persecuted by the Romans for their beliefs but soon merged with them under Constantine, Theodosius and finally the Frankish King Charlemagne. The papal states came into being and no one could see where the spiritual and temporal power began or ended.

The Church, now the keeper of truth and holding the power of the keys, defined dogma, practice, morality and laid down numerous cannon laws. Those who did not obey were persecuted, judged by the Inquisitor and possibly killed.

Some radical changes threatened the Church at the time of Martin Luther due to nationalism, the renaissance, the invention of printing, education and the rise of capitalism. Yet the Church survived, Protestant and Catholic, Greek and Russian Orthodox. Many look upon this as a sign of divine favor. They fail to explain God's will in the division of Christendom, within which all claim they possess the truth and the enforcing power to make it hold.

Today, there is great unrest in the Church and whether it is known or not it is necessary for a new paradigm to emerge that can adequately represent the present time. To use blood letting as a medical practice today would be an affront to all medical knowledge. To use a three thousand year old cosmology to explain the world not only makes us be erroneous but stupid. Yet this same attempt, to use outmoded paradigms, is being continued by the Church.

How threatened leaders are is evidenced by the condemnation of Liberation Theology, the silencing of Leonardo Buff, Tessa Bolasurirja's excommunication and the coldness to Cardinal Bernadine's minor move to get people to dialog. Even this should be forbidden, according to many Cardinals and Bishops.

How can a paradigm that does not include women, gays, married clergy or thinking theologians or thinking lay people, survive as a model in this our winter of discontent?

Maybe many of the women are right. Why should they argue and fight for ordination in a Church that is almost entirely out of step? You cannot take a Model-T Ford and reform it. Can you put an automatic transmission in it, sir conditioning, power-brakes, computers, windshield washers, automatic locks or even add a trunk?

Perhaps the Church cannot be reformed. Vatican II tried it and ever since the full power of the Vatican has effectively stopped it. The Church does not want to be reformed. It is a perfect paradigm, frozen in feudal forms. This paradigm needs to be set aside just like old theories in physics, medicine, car building, house-building and even sports. When the models don't work, can't work they must by shelved, remembered, and studied as history.

This is what must be done now with the Church. People need spiritual renewal, growth, togetherness, focus and the power of the force. Just as we have generated new sources of energy form the water, the wind, the sun and the atom we need to find a new spiritual source of energy in meditation, seeking social justice, ending war, feeding the world and raising humans to be fully human-fully alive. The present Church is not interested and in its limping form cannot get itself off its bed of senescence. The Church is in a rest home.